The
Cold War

OPPOSING
VIEWPOINTS®
DIGESTS

The
Cold War

JAY SPEAKMAN

$$\begin{bmatrix} \textbf{OPPOSING} \\ \textbf{VIEWPOINTS}^{\textcircled{R}} \\ \textbf{DIGESTS} \end{bmatrix}$$

Greenhaven Press, Inc., San Diego, California

Library of Congress Cataloging-in-Publication Data

Speakman, Jay, 1953–
  The Cold War / Jay Speakman.
     p.   cm. — (Opposing viewpoints digests)
Includes bibliographical references and index.
  ISBN 0-7377-0421-7 (hardback : alk. paper) — ISBN 0-7377-0420-9
(pbk. : alk. paper)
  1. Cold War. 2. World politics—1945- 3. International relations.
4. Europe—Politics and government—1945- 5. United States—Foreign
relations—Soviet Union. 6. Soviet Union—Foreign relations—United
States. [1. Cold War. 2. World politics—1945- 3. United States—
Foreign relations—Soviet Union. 4. Soviet Union—Foreign relations—
United States.] I. Title. II. Series.
  D843 .S625 2001
  940.55—dc21
                                                          00-011681

Cover Photo: Peter Turnley/Corbis
Library of Congress: 30, 65, 89
NASA: 41
National Archives: 61
Naval Photographic Center: 32
White House: 82

CONTENTS

FOREWORD

The only way in which a human being can make some approach to knowing the whole of a subject is by hearing what can be said about it by persons of every variety of opinion and studying all modes in which it can be looked at by every character of mind. No wise man ever acquired his wisdom in any mode but this.

—John Stuart Mill

Greenhaven Press's Opposing Viewpoints Digests in history are designed to aid in examining important historical issues in a way that develops critical thinking and evaluating skills. Each book presents thought-provoking argument and stimulating debate on a single topic. In analyzing issues through opposing views, students gain a social and historical context that cannot be discovered in textbooks. Excerpts from primary sources reveal the personal, political, and economic side of historical topics such as the American Revolution, the Great Depression, and the Bill of Rights. Students begin to understand that history is not a dry recounting of facts, but a record founded on ideas—ideas that become manifest through lively discussion and debate. Digests immerse students in contemporary discussions: Why did many colonists oppose a bill of rights? What was the original intent of the New Deal and on what grounds was it criticized? These arguments provide a foundation for students to assess today's debates on censorship, welfare, and other issues. For example, *The Great Depression: Opposing Viewpoints Digests* offers opposing arguments on controversial issues of the time as well as views and interpretations that interest modern historians. A major debate during Franklin D. Roosevelt's administration was whether the president's New Deal programs would lead to a permanent welfare state, creating a citizenry dependent on government money. *The Great Depression* covers this issue from both historical and modern perspectives, allowing students to critically evaluate arguments both in the context of their time and through the benefit of historical hindsight.

This emphasis on debate makes Digests a useful tool for writing reports, research papers, and persuasive essays. In addition to supplying students with a range of possible topics and supporting material, the Opposing Viewpoints Digests offer unique features through which young readers acquire and sharpen critical thinking and reading skills. To assure an appropriate and consistent reading level for young adults, all essays in each volume are written by a single author. Each essay heavily quotes readable primary sources that are fully cited to allow for further research and documentation. Thus, primary sources are introduced in a context to enhance comprehension.

In addition, each volume includes extensive research tools, including a section comprising excerpts from original documents pertaining to the issue under discussion. In *The Bill of Rights*, for example, readers can examine the English Magna Carta, the Virginia State Bill of Rights drawn up in 1776, and various opinions by U.S. Supreme Court justices in key civil rights cases, as well as an unabridged version of the U.S. Bill of Rights. These documents both complement the text and give students access to a wide variety of relevant sources in a single volume. Additionally, a "facts about" section allows students to peruse facts and statistics that pertain to the topic. These statistics are also fully cited, allowing students to question and analyze the credibility of the source. Two bibliographies, one for young adults and one listing the author's sources, are also included; both are annotated to guide student research. Finally, a comprehensive index allows students to scan and locate content efficiently.

Greenhaven's Opposing Viewpoints Digests, like Greenhaven's higher level and critically acclaimed Opposing Viewpoints Series, have been developed around the concept that an awareness and appreciation for the complexity of seemingly simple issues is particularly important in a democratic society. In a democracy, the common good is often, and very appropriately, decided by open debate of widely varying views. As one of democracy's greatest advocates, Thomas Jefferson, observed, "Difference of opinion leads to inquiry, and inquiry to truth." It is to this principle that Opposing Viewpoints Digests are dedicated.

Half a Century of Rivalry Between Superpowers

In 1830 the French political observer Alexis de Tocqueville wrote that two countries, the United States and Russia, seemed fated "by some secret design of Providence one day to hold in its hands the destinies of half the world."[1] A century and a half later, de Tocqueville's fantastic prediction was realized. Vastly more powerful than all other countries, the American and Soviet "superpowers" engaged in a global rivalry that dominated world politics for more than four decades. The rivalry was all the more acute because of the deep ideological divide between the U.S. market-based democracy and the Soviet system of totalitarian Communism, a system characterized by a state-controlled economy and dictatorship by a single party. Because the Cold War coincided with the dawn of the nuclear age, the Soviet-American rivalry was historically unique and uniquely dangerous. Yet the existence of nuclear weapons also forced American and Soviet leaders to temper their competition with caution.

For the sake of convenience, the Cold War can be divided into five phases: the beginning or origins phase, 1945–1950; the phase of deep antagonism, 1950–1962; the moderated rivalry and détente phase, 1963–1973; renewed tensions, 1973–1985; and the end phase, from 1985 to the collapse of the Soviet Union in 1991.

A Conflict of Ideologies

The Cold War has its origins in the 1917 Russian Revolution led by Vladimir Lenin's Bolsheviks, who created the Union of Soviet Socialist Republics (USSR), also called the Soviet Union.

Based on the Communist philosophy of the nineteenth-century German thinker Karl Marx, the new Bolshevik government was hostile to both democracy and capitalism and committed to the abolition of private property. Instead, the Communist Bolsheviks called for state ownership of factories and farms. In keeping with Marx's call for a worldwide Communist revolution, the Soviets provided assistance to revolutionaries attempting to topple governments in other nations.

Thus, the Cold War was, at heart, a conflict of ideologies: Western capitalism versus Soviet Communism. Some in the West admired Communism and hoped for its success. Most, however, viewed the Soviet regime with suspicion. The United States was founded on principles of limited government, and therefore many Americans viewed the Communist ideal of a state-run economy as antithetical to individual liberty. Soviet Communists, on the other hand, believed that capitalism allowed the rich and powerful elite to exploit the average worker.

A Legacy of Distrust

The Soviets' relationship with the West was marked by distrust from the beginning. Coming to power in the midst of World War I, the new Communist regime made a separate peace with imperial Germany, leaving its British, French, and American allies to fight Germany without Russian assistance. Then, in 1918, under complex circumstances, several Western governments sent military forces into Russia during its civil war, leaving a legacy of bitterness and suspicion on the Russian side.

Western governments watched with alarm as the Communists established a tight grip on power, executing Czar Nicholas and his entire family, preserving and expanding the old secret police of the czars, and harshly suppressing all dissent. The dictatorial rule of Joseph Stalin, who took over the Soviet leadership after the death of Lenin, was particularly shocking. The forced takeover of agriculture by the Soviet government (collectivization) caused huge famines and immense suffering, and mass arrests of those who opposed the government were the hallmarks of Stalin's rule.

Western governments were appalled as tens of millions died or were imprisoned in the USSR.

The rise of the Nazis in Germany in the 1930s created problems between the Soviet Union and the West. The Soviets resented the British and French appeasement policy—making many concessions to Germany while failing to respond to Nazi aggressiveness—and Western governments were shocked when Germany and the Soviet Union signed a nonaggression pact in 1939 with a secret agreement to divide Poland. Emboldened by the pact, Germany invaded Poland, starting World War II.

A Temporary Alliance

When Hitler invaded the Soviet Union in 1941, the Soviet Union and Britain became allies, soon to be joined by the United States. The three Allies fought together to victory in World War II but experienced mutual suspicions and frictions throughout the conflict. By war's end, Washington and London were alarmed over Moscow's tendency to grab land from its neighbors and use the war as an excuse to engineer border changes favorable to the Soviet Union.

The Soviet Union's leading role in the defeat of Nazi Germany demonstrated its awesome military prowess. With most of Europe defeated or exhausted, the Communist giant remained as the only European superpower. War's end left many new and unresolved international problems, and the Western powers and the Soviet Union were on opposite sides on almost all of them.

The eighteen months following the end of World War II saw the U.S.-Soviet alliance give way to renewed tensions and mutual suspicions. The most immediate issues concerned the future of Poland and Germany.

Germany was occupied by the victorious powers, with the United States and Britain in the west and the Soviet Union in the east. Similarly, the capital city of Berlin was divided into western and eastern sectors. Washington and Moscow agreed that occupation and division should be temporary and that Germany had to be purged of Nazi influence and militarism. Beyond that, they disagreed. The United States wanted to see a democratic reunified Germany that was militarily weak. The Soviet Union favored German reunification only if Germany were kept weak and susceptible to Soviet influence, preferably Communist. Failing that, the Soviets were determined to maintain strict control over East Germany, which had been transformed into a Communist dictatorship. Unable to negotiate German reunification with the Soviets, the United States and Britain transformed West Germany into a constitutional democracy.

Poland, too, was a bone of contention. The United States and Britain wanted Poland's wartime leaders to organize a temporary government and then hold free elections. They also wanted Polish borders to remain where they had been in 1939. In contrast, the Soviets wanted a government organized around a nucleus of Polish Communists who had spent the war in the USSR. They wanted a Poland friendly to the Soviet Union. And they wanted to move Poland's borders to the west. A compromise was reached at the Yalta conference in early 1945. But over the long term, Yalta produced only disagreement and discord. The Red Army changed Poland's borders, and the West could do little about it. Free elections were never held, and Poland became a Communist country under the near-total influence of the USSR. In the United States, Polish developments produced a marked increase in anti-Soviet anger and suspicions. At the same time, the Soviets were tightening their grip on other Eastern European countries. Britain's former prime minister, Winston Churchill, warned that an "iron curtain" was descending between Eastern and Western Europe.

American fears deepened with other Soviet moves, especially toward countries nearest to the Soviet Union. In a series of incidents, Moscow applied pressure to Turkey and Iran, attempting to take territory or extend Soviet influence over those countries. In early 1947 American leaders saw danger-ous and growing vacuums of power made worse when an impoverished Britain gave up its possessions and responsibili-ties in India, the Middle East, and the eastern Mediterranean. At the same time, a civil war was raging in Greece. It appeared that the Soviets were backing Communist rebels. (In reality, the Soviet Union was scarcely involved; the Communist gov-ernment of Yugoslavia was encouraging and aiding the Greek Communists.) President Harry Truman asked Congress for military aid for Greece and Turkey. In what came to be called the Truman Doctrine, the president declared: "It must be the policy of the United States to support free peoples who are resisting attempted subjugation by armed minorities or by outside pressures."[2] From then until the collapse of the Soviet Union in 1991, containment of Communism would be the cornerstone of American foreign policy.

Tensions worsened in 1948. In Czechoslovakia, the last Eastern European country in which non-Communist parties played any real role in government, Communists staged a coup and established total control. Berlin became the focal point of the most serious confrontation in the early Cold War as the Soviets imposed a blockade of the land routes to the city in response to Western-sponsored currency reform in West Germany. Resisting advice to break the blockade by force, President Truman responded with a massive airlift, supplying the city of 2 million for a year until the Soviets finally relent-ed and lifted the blockade. Because of the blockade, the United States, Canada, and ten European nations formed a military alliance, the North Atlantic Treaty Organization (NATO), in 1949. The division of Europe into hostile camps had become very deep.

In the late summer of 1949, the Soviets set off their first atomic explosion, intensifying Western fears of Soviet power. Just two months later the government of China, the world's most populous country, fell to Communist revolutionaries led by Mao Tse-tung. In early 1950 the two Communist

giants became military allies. In June 1950 Communist North Korea invaded non-Communist South Korea with the encouragement and support of China and the Soviet Union. The United States intervened, waging the costly Korean War for three years.

Deep Hostility: 1950–1963

Following the Chinese Revolution and the onset of the Korean War, the United States entered into a number of alliances and defense agreements and nearly quadrupled its defense budget. West Germany was rearmed and brought into NATO. In retaliation, the Soviet Union forged a military alliance, known as the Warsaw Pact, with its six Eastern European neighbors (East Germany, Poland, Hungary, Czechoslovakia, Romania, Bulgaria, and for a short time Albania).

The death of Stalin in 1953 brought a slight thaw. The Soviets made some positive moves in Europe, and in 1955 President Dwight Eisenhower held a summit conference in Geneva with Soviet leaders. Though not very productive, the meeting was cordial and for some time afterward newspapers wrote about the cooperative spirit of Geneva. In 1956 Soviet leader Nikita Khrushchev generated hopes for domestic and

Europe During the Cold War

Denmark

USSR

Netherlands

Britain

Berlin

Belgium

East
Germany

Poland

Luxembourg

West
Germany

Czechoslovakia

Switzerland

Austria

Hungary

France

Italy

Romania

Yugoslavia

Spain

Soviet-controlled
Eastern Europe

Albania

international changes by denouncing Stalin's crimes and stating that war between East and West was not inevitable.

Nonetheless, the rivalry remained intense. Soviet influence in Asia and the Middle East grew, and Soviet domination of Eastern Europe remained intact. In 1957 the USSR succeeded in putting two Sputnik satellites in space, raising fears in the United States that the Soviets were on the verge of developing rockets capable of striking the United States with nuclear warheads. Khrushchev bragged that the Soviets would turn out nuclear missiles like sausages, and Democratic presidential contender John F. Kennedy accused the Eisenhower administration of allowing a missile gap to develop. All the while, Moscow's Chinese allies remained bitterly anti-American and became involved with the United States in two dangerous crises over small islands under the control of Beijing's rivals in Taiwan.

In 1961 the new American president, John F. Kennedy, was greeted with a crisis in West Berlin: To prevent East Germans from escaping to West Germany, the Soviet Union ordered the building of the Berlin Wall, which served as a symbol of the division between Eastern and Western Europe until 1989. In 1962 Kennedy confronted the most dangerous crisis of the Cold War when the Soviets secretly deployed nuclear missiles on the island of Cuba, just ninety miles from the U.S. coast. Kennedy threatened nuclear retaliation. After a U.S. naval blockade of Cuba and intense secret negotiations, the Soviets agreed to withdraw the missiles, ending the tense thirteen-day crisis that seemed to bring the world to brink of nuclear war.

Moderated Rivalry and Détente, 1963–1973

The crises in Berlin and Cuba demonstrated just how dangerous the intense superpower rivalry could be, giving both countries an incentive to relax tensions. In 1963 a conciliatory speech by Kennedy was soon followed by direct negotiations between the superpowers, leading to the crisis-management hot line between Washington and Moscow and to the Partial Test Ban Treaty, which prohibited nuclear tests above ground and under the sea.

The general move toward improved relations was sidetracked, however, by the 1963 assassination of President Kennedy and by America's growing involvement in Vietnam. U.S. leaders were also dismayed in 1968 by Moscow's invasion of Czechoslovakia for the purpose of crushing that country's experiment in trying to institute a more humane form of Communism.

The high point in East-West relations soon followed, however. In Europe, agreements about Berlin and negotiations to achieve limits on conventional weapons were concluded. The Soviet Union and several Eastern European states signed peace agreements with Germany, the first since World War II. An elaborate treaty addressing security issues, human rights, and increased intercourse between East and West, called the Helsinki Accords, was signed in 1975.

U.S.-Soviet relations moved in the same direction. Ironically, President Richard Nixon, who had a reputation as an arch anti-Communist, was the architect of the agreements that produced a new era of relaxed tensions, called détente. The centerpiece of détente was a Strategic Arms Limitation Talks (SALT) accord capping the numbers of nuclear delivery systems and severely limiting antiballistic missiles. The superpowers also concluded a trade agreement and several minor treaties. All of these agreements were signed at a summit meeting, held with great fanfare in Moscow in 1972, between Nixon and Soviet leader Leonid Brezhnev.

Renewed Tensions

The euphoria of détente did not last long. The United States was turning inward as a result of Vietnam. The Soviet Union, in contrast, embarked on a major across-the-board military buildup matched by concerted efforts to expand its influence around the world. Détente was strained to the breaking point by Moscow's global activism and Washington's anger over what it perceived as deliberate moves by the Soviets to take advantage of America's global retreat.

Thus, as Stanley Hoffmann, a scholar of European affairs at Harvard, notes, "There were less than three good years"[3] of détente between the superpowers. Barely a year after the Moscow summit, détente was shaken by the outbreak of a fourth Middle Eastern war. Before and during the 1973 Arab-Israeli conflict, the Soviets provided large stocks of weapons to the Arab belligerents, enabling them to score impressive early gains against the Israelis. The Nixon administration accused the Soviets of failing to inform Washington of the coming conflict or acting to halt it. The conflict became a superpower crisis when the Soviets threatened to intervene with their own forces and the United States responded with a low-level nuclear alert.

The crisis helped doom the already troubled U.S.-Soviet trade agreement, détente's biggest attraction for the Soviets. Congress made liberalized trade subject to Soviet steps to permit increased Jewish emigration from the USSR. Although the Nixon administration opposed the congressional action, called the Jackson-Vanik Amendment, Congress was in no mood to grant trade benefits to the Soviets after the 1973 war.

Soviet activism outside of Europe was a central issue in U.S.-Soviet relations in the 1970s and 1980s. As W. Raymond Duncan and Carolyn McGiffert Ekedahl note in *Moscow and the Third World Under Gorbachev*, "The U.S.S.R. experienced the greatest expansion of its position in the Third World in the mid to late 1970s, when pro-Soviet regimes came to power in Angola, Ethiopia, Grenada, Nicaragua, and Afghanistan," as well as Vietnam, Laos, and Cambodia. As a result, Duncan and Ekedahl contend, the Soviets "significantly enhanced their power projection and intelligence gathering capabilities in the Third World, gathering access to air and naval facilities in a number of countries."[4]

In late 1979 the Soviets conducted their first ever large-scale military intervention outside the Warsaw Pact area, sending fifty-thousand troops into Afghanistan to combat an Islamic uprising against that country's Communist government. It was a watershed, marking a clear transition from détente to a renewal of the Cold War. Deeply angered, President Jimmy Carter imposed an array of economic sanctions on the Soviet Union and announced that the United States would boycott the 1980 Olympics in Moscow. Carter stepped up U.S. military spending, created a Rapid Deployment Force for operations in the Persian Gulf region, and began providing covert assistance to the Islamic rebels in Afghanistan. The United States also improved relations with China, which the Soviets found threatening (throughout the 1960s, in the so-called Sino-Soviet split, the Soviet Union and China had gone from being allies to bitter enemies).

At the same time, the Soviets were deploying new intermediate-range nuclear forces (INF) directed at Western Europe, which NATO members saw as instruments of political intimidation and as weapons that could enable the USSR to wage a limited nuclear war against Europe.

The Soviets were also actively expanding and modernizing their strategic nuclear forces targeted on the United States. Conservatives accused the Soviets of violating the terms of the SALT agreements. In 1979 Carter had completed a SALT II accord with the Soviets, but it faced intense opposition in the Senate, where the president's critics claimed that the treaty favored the Soviets and undercut U.S. security. Afghanistan effectively killed the treaty.

The 1980 presidential election was won by Ronald Reagan, who had long been known for his pronounced anti-Communist views. Few were surprised by his escalation of anti-Soviet rhetoric or appointment of hard-liners to the cabinet. Calling the Soviet Union an "evil empire," Reagan accused Soviet leaders of being willing "to commit any crime, to lie, to cheat"[5] to advance the cause of Communism. In 1983, when the Soviets mistook a Korean Airlines passenger aircraft for a spy plane and shot it down, killing 267 people, Reagan condemned the Soviet action, calling it an "act of barbarism" and a "crime against humanity."[6]

In December 1981, under pressure from Moscow, the Polish government cracked down on a newly formed independent trade union called Solidarity. Solidarity leaders were arrested, and martial law was declared. Reflecting deep and widespread American sympathy for the Poles, President Reagan strongly denounced the Soviets and imposed new sanctions.

In 1983 the Soviets harshly criticized Reagan for proposing his Strategic Defense Initiative, a grandiose plan for developing defenses against missiles, which Moscow claimed would threaten the integrity of its retaliatory nuclear capability.

The End of the Cold War

The early 1980s brought one contentious issue after another, and these years also witnessed instability at the top of the Soviet government. Three successive aged leaders died in four years. During this period of leadership flux and uncertainty, Soviet foreign policy was all but paralyzed. Bold initiatives to break the deadlock with the United States were not possible.

Things changed dramatically with the selection of Mikhail Gorbachev as first secretary of the Communist Party in March 1985. Sobered by the serious problems afflicting the Soviet economy (slow growth, technological backwardness, and severe shortages of goods), the new leader was drawn to proposals for radical reform. In sharp departures from Communist orthodoxy, Gorbachev invited greater openness (glasnost) in political debate and participation and called for restructuring (perestroika) of the Soviet economy.

In the first three years of his leadership Gorbachev was tentative about making changes in foreign policy. On the major issues, there was more continuity than change. But Gorbachev realized the Soviet Union was overextended internationally and needed good relations with the United States in order to increase needed flows of trade and concentrate on domestic reform. By 1990 Gorbachev had agreed to ambitious INF and Strategic Arms Reduction Talks (START) treaties and a treaty requiring large reductions of Soviet armored forces in Europe. He negotiated an end to the Soviet war in Afghanistan. He supported international mediation to end civil wars in Africa, Asia, and Central America, leading to the fall of pro-Soviet governments. He drastically cut economic aid and military support to Soviet client states.

His most dramatic reform was to announce that the Red Army would no longer maintain Soviet domination or keep repressive regimes in power in Eastern Europe. In short order, the Berlin Wall was breached and one Communist regime after another toppled. In the face of firm pressures from President George Bush, Gorbachev even reconciled himself to a reunified Germany in NATO in return for reassurances about Soviet security needs and generous offers of aid.

With the fall of the Berlin Wall and the agreement to reunify Germany, the Cold War was effectively over. The definitive end came when an attempted coup against Gorbachev by hard-line Communists in August 1991 failed, leading to the demise of Soviet Communism. This in turn triggered the breakup of the Soviet Union itself. A democrat, Boris Yeltsin, came to power in the new non-Communist Russia, the principal successor state to the USSR. With its military spending severely cut and only half the population of the former Soviet Union, Russia was no longer a superpower.

Looking Back

A major era in contemporary history was truly over. But it did not pass easily or without real risk of conflict. For almost half a century, American decision makers confronted numerous dilemmas about how to meet the Soviet challenge. In turn, the tactics and aims behind America's defense and foreign policies toward the Soviet Union created many controversies. *Opposing Viewpoints Digests: The Cold War* explores the policies that the United States pursued in over four decades of conflict with the Soviet Union.

1. Alexis de Tocqueville, *Democracy in America*, trans. George Lawrence. New York: Harper and Row, 1969, p. 413.
2. Quoted in Cecil V. Crabb Jr., *The Doctrines of American Foreign Policy: Their Meaning, Role, and Future*. Baton Rouge: Louisiana State University Press, 1982, p. 136.
3. Quoted in Joseph S. Nye Jr., ed., *The Making of America's Soviet Policy*. New Haven, CT: Yale University Press, 1984, p. 231.
4. W. Raymond Duncan and Carolyn McGiffert Ekedahl, *Moscow and the Third World Under Gorbachev*. Boulder, CO: Westview, 1990, pp. 34, 35.
5. Quoted in Thomas G. Paterson, J. Garry Clifford, and Kenneth J. Hagan, *American Foreign Relations: A History*. 4th ed. Lexington, MA: D.C. Heath, 1995, p. 508.
6. Quoted in Ralph B. Levering, *The Cold War, 1945–1987*. Arlington Heights, IL: Harlan Davidson, 1988, p. 173; Paterson, Clifford, and Hagan, *American Foreign Relations*, pp. 517–18.

CHAPTER 1

Origins of the Cold War

"Faced with Moscow's belligerent and threatening behavior, Western nations had no choice but to create a defensive alliance."

The Soviet Union Was to Blame for the Cold War

At the end of World War II, the United States and other Western powers hoped to maintain good relations with the Soviet Union. Sadly, it was not to be. Instead, East-West relations were soon marked by mistrust, tension, and a constant danger of war. The fault rested entirely with the Soviet Union.

Led by a paranoid and dangerous Communist dictator, Joseph Stalin, the Soviet Union oppressed its own people and menaced its neighbors. In the five-year period following World War II, the USSR took a number of hostile actions and refused to cooperate with the West to find solutions to the numerous problems created by the war against Germany. The United States could do nothing to change Soviet hostility. Instead, the United States had to ensure that the Soviet Union's aggressive behavior did not harm American interests or world peace.

Tracing the Cold War to the Russian Revolution

From the start, the Soviet regime was a regime of thugs. Czar Nicholas and his entire family were murdered by the Bolsheviks. The Soviets imposed a frightful tyranny of one-party rule.

Critics of the regime were called insects, fit only for jail or exter-mination. Instead of saving the working man from the exploita-tion of capitalism, Communism created terrible new exploiters and succeeded only in creating an equality of poverty (except for the privileged Communist elite).

Under Joseph Stalin, the reign of terror was almost unimaginable. Between 1929 and 1933 Stalin collectivized agriculture, fulfilling a grim Communist goal and creating a so-called terror-famine to extinguish nationalist sentiment in the Ukrainian Republic. The human suffering was incalcula-ble. As scholar Robert Conquest explains, "The number dying in Stalin's war against the peasants was higher than the total deaths for all countries in World War I."[1]

Paranoid over any possible threat to his rule, Stalin launched the Great Terror (also called the purges) of 1936–1938; thousands of loyal Communists were arrested, and the highest ranks of the Soviet military were almost com-pletely eliminated. More than a million people were executed. Millions more were tortured, jailed, or sent to Siberian prison camps. Most of the prison inmates perished, their deaths "caused by unbearable toil, cold and starvation, by unheard of degradation and humiliation, by a life which could not have been endured by any other mammal,"[2] as an article published in the Soviet Union later acknowledged.

Cruel at home, the Communists were also dangerous abroad. Upon coming to power, the Communist regime fla-grantly violated international law by refusing to pay debts to Western creditors and by confiscating foreign assets without providing compensation. In the midst of World War I, the Communist government cynically abandoned its allies (Britain, France, and the United States), leaving them to fight imperial Germany alone.

Soviet leader Vladimir Lenin himself openly declared that "the existence of the Soviet Republic side by side with the imperialist states for a prolonged period of time is unthink-able. In the meantime a series of frightful collisions will occur."[3] The Soviets routinely aided revolutionaries attempting to topple other governments.

Irresponsible Soviet behavior helped cause World War II. In 1939 Stalin made a stunning and cynical decision to sign a nonaggression pact with Adolf Hitler allowing the Nazis to direct their aggression westward. The Nazis then attacked Poland, causing World War II. In 1941 the USSR signed a treaty of neutrality with Japan that had similar results, encouraging Japan to attack the United States at Pearl Harbor later in the year.

Soviet Hostility to the West After the War

Soviet diplomats were rude and uncooperative at the various postwar international conferences that addressed the numerous problems left by the war. The United States tried to create a stable and secure international order and to ease human suffering in war-torn Europe. The Soviet Union, on the other hand, tried to expand its influence and its control of territory, revealing it to be the successor to Nazi Germany as the biggest threat to international peace and security.

At war's end, the United States rapidly demobilized troops and decommissioned weapons. The Soviet Union did not. Even after the defeat of the Nazis, the Soviet Union continued to field a huge, threatening army—one that it did not need and could ill afford. In early 1946 Stalin made a major speech declaring that the economy and society of the Soviet Union would remain militarized for a long time to come. He strongly suggested that the USSR anticipated another world war, with Western democracies as the enemy. With the intensity of religious fanatics, Stalin and his subordinates believed in the "Marxian theory of ultimate destruction of capitalist states by communist states,"[4] as a 1946 report to President Harry Truman concluded.

American leaders correctly believed that, as Pulitzer Prize–winning author Daniel Yergin puts it, "domestic Soviet totalitarianism inevitably meant a totalitarian foreign policy—

that is, a foreign policy motivated primarily by ideology and geared to unlimited expansion and the complete domination of the international system."[5] As the earlier experience with Hitler indicated, a dictatorship willing to oppress its own people was unlikely to have much respect for the freedom and independence of other countries or for world peace. Additionally, a regime based on terror needed a foreign enemy to keep its people in line.

Stalin was cunning and patient, not reckless like Hitler. As the distinguished diplomat and Sovietologist George Kennan warned, the Soviet Union's "political action is a fluid stream which moves constantly, wherever it is permitted to move, toward a given goal. Its main concern is to make sure that it has filled every nook and cranny available to it in the basin of world power."[6] The first nooks and crannies were found in Eastern Europe, and Stalin wasted little time in filling them.

Soviet Misbehavior in Poland and Eastern Europe

Like the czars of old, Stalin viewed Eastern Europe in general and Poland in particular as territory to be conquered by the Russians. When Germany invaded western Poland in 1939, the Soviet Union invaded and occupied eastern Poland—two vultures feeding on the carcass of the Polish nation. Stalin's ruthlessness was further demonstrated when Soviet troops murdered roughly fifteen-thousand Polish officers and other soldiers in a cruel attempt to shape Poland by exterminating its future leaders.

Toward the end of the war, the Soviets lured the Poles into rising up against the Nazis with promises of support. When fighting ensued, write James A. Nathan and James K. Oliver in their book *United States Foreign Policy and World Order*, the Soviet Red Army sat and watched "as the Nazis liquidated the last vestiges of any potential opposition to Soviet domination of the future government of Poland."[7] While a quarter million Poles perished and Warsaw was destroyed, Stalin even refused landing rights to Western planes seeking to drop supplies to the Poles.

After the war, the Red Army forcibly incorporated part of eastern Poland into the USSR. Despite agreeing to free elections and a democratic future for Poland, Stalin went back on his word. The Red Army installed an unpopular Communist regime in Poland, and free elections were never held. Poland's Communist government established a police state modeled after Moscow's, and Poland became a satellite country under the near-total influence of the Soviet Union.

Between 1945 and 1948 the Polish pattern was repeated throughout Eastern Europe. An iron curtain cut through the heart of Europe as Poland, Czechoslovakia, Hungary, Romania, Bulgaria, and Albania all became Communized, repressive police states dancing to the beat of the Soviet master. The Soviet Union "had simply swallowed up half of Europe,"[8] as scholar Louis J. Halle writes. This was bad enough, but Western nations worried that, given the chance, Stalin might swallow the other half.

The Soviet Threat to Western Europe

Stalin openly admired Czar Alexander I, whose troops reached all the way to Paris after the Napoleonic wars. But the Soviet threat to a weakened Western Europe was not just military. The Soviet Communist Party had deep influence over a number of youth organizations, unions, publishers, religious societies, and political groups in the West. Several European countries had powerful Communist parties that were obedient to Moscow. For good reason, President Truman feared that "the seeds of totalitarian regimes are nurtured by misery and want. They spread and grow in the evil soil of poverty and strife."[9] Following the destruction of World War II, there was plenty of evil soil in Europe, and the Soviets could plant many seeds. There was also a focal point for East-West friction in Europe: Germany.

The German Issue

Because of its economic and industrial might and its military potential, Germany was critical for the future peace and prosperity of Europe. The United States favored a Germany that was unified and democratic, economically strong, but militarily weak. Under American occupation, West Germany was given humanitarian aid and was transformed into a constitutional democracy.

The Soviet view and approach were quite different. In East Germany, the Soviets imposed a Communist dictatorship backed by the Red Army and a powerful secret police. The Soviets wanted to keep East Germany under Communist control and would not accept reunification unless Germany were left very weak and susceptible to Soviet influence. Thus, the Soviets refused to cooperate in the search for a just solution to the German problem, and Soviet power posed a constant threat to West Germany.

In 1948 the threat worsened when the Soviets imposed a military blockade on West Berlin. Stalin intended to starve a city of 2 million free citizens into submission, despite his earlier pledge to respect the West's right to use access corridors across East Germany to reach West Berlin. The move appeared to be a test of the West's will. If the Soviets were allowed to take Berlin, they might have then moved against West Germany and perhaps all of Western Europe. Truman saved the beleaguered city and demonstrated American resolve by undertaking a massive yearlong airlift of supplies to Berlin. By employing an airlift instead of using force to open the land routes, he avoided war. Faced with Moscow's belligerent and threatening behavior, Western nations had no choice but to create a defensive alliance. In 1949 the United States, Canada, and ten European nations created the North Atlantic Treaty Organization (NATO) to protect peace and security in Europe.

A Pattern of Soviet Belligerence

In addition to dominating Eastern Europe and threatening Western Europe, the Soviets sought to expand their influence in Asia and the oil-rich Middle East. Stalin revived and renamed the Lenin-era Communist International, a global net-work of Communist parties following Moscow's leadership and promoting anti-Western activities worldwide. The Soviets operated large spy networks in North America and Europe. In 1949, they successfully tested an atomic weapon; nuclear weapons were then in the hands of the ruthless leaders of the world's greatest land power. The Communist threat increased in 1949 and 1950 when China, the world's most populous coun-try, fell to Communism and shortly afterward allied itself to the USSR. Then, in June 1950, Communist North Korea invaded non-Communist South Korea with evident Soviet and Chinese connivance. The Cold War had spread across the entire globe, and it had become very intense and dangerous.

1. Robert Conquest, *The Harvest of Sorrow: Soviet Collectivization and the Terror-Famine.* New York: Oxford University Press, 1986, p. 4.

2. Quoted in Robert Conquest, *The Great Terror: A Reassessment.* New York: Oxford University Press, 1990, p. 339.

3. Quoted in James A. Nathan and James K. Oliver, *United States Foreign Policy and World Order.* 4th ed. Glenview, IL: Scott, Foresman, 1989, p. 12.

4. Quoted in Melvyn P. Leffler, *A Preponderance of Power: National Security, the Truman Administration, and the Cold War.* Palo Alto, CA: Stanford University Press, 1992, p. 131.

5. Daniel Yergin, *Shattered Peace: The Origins of the Cold War and the National Security State.* Boston: Houghton Mifflin, 1977, p. 222.

6. Mr. X (George Kennan), "The Sources of Soviet Conduct," *Foreign Affairs*, Spring 1987, p. 861.

7. Nathan and Oliver, *United States Foreign Policy and World Order*, p. 28.

8. Louis J. Halle, *The Cold War as History.* New York: Harper, 1967, p. 1.

9. Quoted in Thomas G. Paterson and Dennis Merrill, eds., *Major Problems in American Foreign Relations: Documents and Essays.* 4th ed. Lexington, MA: D.C. Heath, 1995, p. 261.

"The Cold War occurred because the United States made unrealistic and unreasonable demands on the Soviets, misinterpreted Soviet behavior, and exaggerated the Soviet 'threat.'"

The United States Was to Blame for the Cold War

At the end of World War II, the Soviet Union was in shambles. Much of the USSR's industry and economy was wrecked. The death toll of war was ghastly: Twenty million Soviet citizens were dead; roughly fifty Russians for every American who died. The last thing Moscow wanted was another war. Even Adam B. Ulam, a scholar who was very critical of the Soviets, admits that a military clash with the United States "was simply inconceivable to a man as realistic and cautious as Stalin."[1]

From 1941 on, fully 80 percent of Germany's military power was directed to the war against the USSR. Despite the USSR's great contribution to the Allied victory, achieved at dreadful cost, Soviet needs and desires in the postwar world received little sympathy and understanding from the West. Early Western policies left a legacy of mistrust and suspicion in Moscow that helped cause the Cold War.

Moscow's Earlier Grievances

The Western powers had been hostile to the Bolshevik government from the start, mounting two interventions in the Soviet Union in support of the Communists' enemies within three years of the 1917 revolution. British prime minister Winston Churchill openly regretted that the West had missed the opportunity to strangle the Bolshevik baby in the cradle. Until 1933, the United States had refused even to maintain diplomatic relations with the Communist regime.

In the 1930s, when the Soviet Union faced a growing threat from Nazi Germany, France and Britain refused to align with the Soviet Union against Germany. Instead, they appeased the Nazis, doing nothing when Germany remilitarized the Rhineland in 1936, annexed Austria in 1938, and took first part, and then all, of Czechoslovakia in 1938 and 1939. The Western powers virtually invited Germany to direct its aggressive energies toward the Soviet Union.

(Left to right) World War II Allied leaders Joseph Stalin, Franklin D. Roosevelt, and Winston Churchill at the Tehran Conference in Tehran, Iran, in 1943.

In 1941 Hitler did just that, invading the USSR. Many in the West shared the cynical sentiment of Senator Harry Truman (who would become U.S. president four years later), who welcomed war between Germany and the USSR, even suggesting that the United States should help whichever side was losing "and that way let them kill as many [of each other] as possible."[2]

The Soviet Union desperately needed Britain and the United States to land armies in Western Europe to draw some of Germany's fighting strength away from the USSR. For three long years, Stalin's pleas for a second front in Europe fell on deaf ears. The United States also kept its Soviet allies in the dark about the development of the atomic bomb even though it shared some information about the project with the British.

With Germany's surrender in 1945, Truman abruptly canceled America's military assistance program (called Lend-Lease) to the USSR. Shortly after the war, the United States offered an immense loan to Great Britain, but it offered nothing to the Soviet Union.

The USSR in 1945: Alone in a Hostile World

Western actions before and during World War II left a legacy of distrust and suspicion in Moscow. But it was the confrontational attitude of the United States under the leadership of inexperienced President Truman after the war that produced the deep freeze known as the Cold War.

At the end of World War II the Soviets, not the West, had reason to fear the other side. The United States, not the Soviet Union, had the atomic bomb and had demonstrated at Hiroshima and Nagasaki that it was willing to use it. In fact, when the United States dropped the bombs on Japan, its real aim may have been to intimidate the Soviet Union rather than to defeat Japan, which was virtually powerless and on the verge of surrender. After the defeat of the Fascist powers, the United States maintained its

A 1945 photo of Hiroshima, Japan, shows the damage caused by the United States' atomic bombs.

monopoly of atomic weapons and increased the size of its nuclear arsenal.

While the Soviet Union was devastated by World War II, the United States was untouched. In fact, America's economy and industrial might had grown rapidly during the war years. American territory was safe and secure. In contrast, the massive territory of the Soviet Union was sprawled out across the heartland of Europe and Asia, vulnerable to invasion from almost every direction. Russia also had a long history of invasions—by Mongols, Turks, Swedes, Poles, the French, and Germans.

The Soviet Union was alone in an unfriendly world. Of the world's five major centers of power or potential power, four were lined up together against the USSR: the United States, Western Europe, Japan, and China. The West was dominant in the rest of the world as well. American influence was at an all-time high, and it was buttressed by a large network of military bases all around the world—bases that could be used for attacks against the USSR.

Exaggerating the Soviet Threat

Despite its great power and influence, the United States claimed to be frightened of the Soviet Union. But such fears, if real, were based on persistent exaggerations. Washington overestimated the size of the Soviet Union's postwar armed forces. The Truman administration exaggerated the Soviet threat in the eastern Mediterranean to win congressional approval for the harshly anti-Soviet Truman Doctrine, which called for U.S. aid to anti-Communist forces in Greece and Turkey. Later the Truman Doctrine was expanded to justify support for any nation the United States believed was threatened by Communism. In a key 1950 document that shaped U.S. policy, the USSR's global influence and its potential for developing a war-winning nuclear force by the mid-1950s were grossly exaggerated. At the same time, "any signs of Soviet concessions or willingness to compromise were suspect and to be rejected," according to Daniel Yergin, who notes that in 1947 Truman virtually ignored examples of "seemingly moderate and conciliatory Soviet behavior"[3] cited by his Central Intelligence Agency. It was a pattern to be repeated throughout the Cold War.

U.S. Provocations Toward the Soviet Union

As Ralph B. Levering finds in his study of the Cold War, one of the five main tendencies in Truman's Soviet policy was "an apparent unwillingness to explore seriously with Russia possible areas of compromise"[4] on major issues. The name of the game was getting tough with Moscow. Truman's own commerce secretary, Henry Wallace, warned that getting tough "never brought anything real and lasting—whether for schoolyard bullies or businessmen or world powers. The tougher we get, the tougher the Russians."[5] But Truman did get tough, and relations spiraled downward.

In Western and Eastern Europe and in Asia, the United States tried to dictate the terms of postwar arrangements to Moscow. The United States used a massive program of foreign aid to Europe, the Marshall Plan, as a weapon against the Soviet Union. The Marshall Plan cemented American influence over Western Europe and threatened American penetration into Eastern Europe, the very doorstep of the USSR.

Poland and Eastern Europe

It is true that the Soviets were heavy-handed, even brutal, in their treatment of Eastern Europe. But Soviet actions stemmed from fear and insecurity, not aggressiveness. Poland's flat terrain offered no resistance against the tidal wave of German tanks that invaded the Soviet Union in 1941. The Soviet Union needed a weak buffer zone in Eastern Europe, the one region in the world where the USSR had greater influence than the Western powers. Because Eastern Europeans were historically unfriendly to Moscow, the only way to ensure that Eastern Europe would not be used as a platform for the invasion of the USSR was to install Communist governments there and to dominate the region.

Secretary Wallace warned the president that the United States had no reason to get involved in Eastern Europe and that American efforts to create democracies in Eastern Europe, "where democracy by and large has never existed, seems to [the Soviet Union] an attempt to re-establish the encirclement of unfriendly neighbors which was created after the last war and which might serve as a springboard of still another effort to destroy her."[6]

American concern for the fate of Eastern Europe was hypocritical—and maybe even insincere. American leaders complained about Soviet domination and Communist oppression in Eastern Europe, but the United States had a secure sphere of influence in Latin America, and it did not hesitate to send in the gunboats to keep its neighbors in line. Nor did the United States care much if right-wing but pro-U.S. dictators abused human rights in Nicaragua and elsewhere in the Americas.

Roosevelt and Truman did not really care about Poland. They cared about votes—the votes of several million Americans of Polish origin who were heavily concentrated in key states in the Midwest. Roosevelt and Truman pandered to their intense anti-Sovietism by making an issue of Yalta and Poland.

Germany

In the dispute over Eastern Europe, the United States exaggerated the Soviet threat and acted in ways that were *potentially* threatening to the Soviet Union. In the dispute over Germany, American policy *did* threaten Soviet security.

Twice in thirty years Germany had brought suffering and ruin to Russia. In the years after the war, the Soviet Union simply wanted compensation from Germany for its immense suffering between 1941 and 1945. And Moscow wanted security. It wanted to make sure that Germany would remain too weak to pose a mortal threat yet again to the Soviet Union. Moscow was especially fearful of a combination of American and German power since two-thirds of the population, industry, and territory of Germany were in the Western zone, under control of the Americans and the British.

No solution to the German problem was possible until Moscow had ironclad guarantees that Germany would not rearm and that it would not align itself with the West. But events rapidly moved in the opposite direction. American efforts to democratize West Germany and to rehabilitate its economy could only be seen by the Soviets as an attempt to strengthen it and make it an American ally. The 1948 blockade of Berlin was not an aggressive move toward Western Europe but rather an expression of alarm over American actions that were increasingly drawing West Germany and the rest of Europe into the American orbit of influence. Moscow had no choice but to maintain its hold on East Germany.

Soviet fears of American intentions were not fanciful. In 1949, just four years after the war, the United States allowed West Germany to regain its independence. That same year the United States created the North Atlantic Treaty Organization (NATO), an American military beachhead in Europe. Four years later a rearmed West Germany entered

NATO. More than anything the Soviets did, these actions permanently divided Europe into two mutually suspicious armed camps.

In summary, the Cold War occurred because the United States made unrealistic and unreasonable demands on the Soviets, misinterpreted Soviet behavior, and exaggerated the Soviet "threat."

1. Adam B. Ulam, *Expansion and Coexistence: Soviet Foreign Policy, 1917–73*, 2nd ed. New York: Praeger, 1974, p. 414.

2. Quoted in David McCullough, *Truman*. New York: Touchstone, 1992, p. 262.

3. Daniel Yergin, *Shattered Peace: The Origins of the Cold War and the National Security State*. Boston: Houghton Mifflin, 1977, p. 276.

4. Ralph B. Levering, *The Cold War, 1945–1987*. Arlington Heights, IL: Harlan Davidson, 1988, p. 33.

5. Quoted in Thomas G. Paterson, J. Garry Clifford, and Kenneth J. Hagan, *American Foreign Relations: A History*. 4th ed. Lexington, MA: D.C. Heath, 1995, p. 284.

6. "Henry Wallace Questions the 'Get Tough' Policy, 1946," in Paterson and Merrill, eds. *Major Problems in American Foreign Relations*. Lexington, MA: D.C. Heath, 1995, p. 252.

Cold War Strategies

"The weapons of war must be abolished before they abolish us."

U.S. Nuclear Policies Were Dangerous and Immoral

Throughout the Cold War, the terrible mushroom-shaped cloud of nuclear armageddon hung over all of humanity. The American nuclear strikes against Hiroshima and Nagasaki at the end of World War II inaugurated the nuclear age and at the same time marked the beginning of a dangerous addiction to nuclear weapons that has afflicted American foreign policy ever since.

From the very outset of Cold War hostilities, the United States relied much too heavily on nuclear weapons to accomplish its foreign-policy goals. As a result, even minor clashes and confrontations between the superpowers ran the risk of sparking a catastrophic nuclear war. The United States also accumulated a grotesquely large nuclear arsenal, far larger than was necessary to maintain deterrence.

Extended Deterrence: The Folly of Using Nuclear Weapons as Tools of Foreign Policy

The only thing nuclear weapons are good for is deterring an adversary from using nuclear weapons. The respected strategist Bernard Brodie recognized this in 1946: "Thus far the chief purpose of our military establishment has been to win wars. From now on its chief purpose must be to avert them."[1]

Yet the United States consistently sought to get more out of its nuclear arsenal, extending deterrence to protect other countries against Communist aggression, whether nuclear or nonnuclear.

The administration of President Dwight Eisenhower foolishly made such extended deterrence a main plank of its foreign policy in the strategy of massive retaliation. Under massive retaliation, even minor acts of aggression or Communist-inspired revolutions might trigger thunderous retaliation by America's dreadful and deadly nuclear arsenal. Very early in the Cold War it might have been possible to argue that extended deterrence made some sense since the United States had a virtual monopoly on nuclear striking power. But that monopoly was fleeting. By the time massive retaliation became declared U.S. policy in 1954, Americans were already deeply worried about the growing Soviet nuclear arsenal. A year later they were fretting about a disadvantageous bomber gap (which proved nonexistent) that threatened to give the Soviets nuclear superiority.

As many critics recognized even then, massive retaliation was ineffective because it was not credible. Who could believe that the United States would actually use nuclear weapons in response to, say, Soviet pressure on West Berlin or Communist revolutions in the Third World? In fact, the United States did not use nuclear weapons when Fidel Castro's Communists took power in Cuba or when Vietnamese Communists took power in North Vietnam, showing that massive retaliation was a sham.

Massive retaliation was also dangerous and immoral. It threatened to turn small brushfire conflicts into nuclear conflagrations. Twice in the 1950s, the Eisenhower administration made vague nuclear threats against China in the midst of crises growing out of disputes over Pacific Islands under the control of Taiwan, an ally of the United States. President Eisenhower was lucky. China did back down, but what would have happened if it had not? China did not have nuclear weapons, but it had a radical Communist government willing to take big risks and a nuclear-armed ally, the Soviet Union. Risking a catastrophic nuclear war over tiny, strategically worthless islands was both reckless and immoral.

President John F. Kennedy abandoned massive retaliation, but the strategy that replaced it, flexible response, suffered the same fatal defect: It treated nuclear weapons as if they were just like other weapons. Devised as a strategy to protect Western Europe from Soviet aggression, flexible response committed the United States to using nuclear weapons in a conflict in Europe, even if the Soviets were to attack with only conventional forces. Flexible response envisioned more inter-mediate steps than massive retaliation, with American nuclear strikes against Soviet territory coming only as the last resort. But both strategies allowed for the possibility that the United States would be the first to use nuclear weapons in a crisis.

By the time Kennedy became president, the Soviet Union had nuclear-tipped intercontinental-range nuclear weapons capable of reaching the United States in thirty minutes. The Soviet arsenal only grew thereafter, ensuring that the protective nuclear umbrella the United States offered its allies was poten-tially suicidal for the United States. As four highly respected former U.S. diplomats claimed, "Any use of nuclear weapons in Europe, by the Alliance [NATO] or against it, carries with it a high and inescapable risk of escalation into the general nuclear war which would bring ruin to all and victory to none."[2] Incredibly, even after the Soviet Union achieved nuclear parity with the United States, the U.S. policy of extended deterrence never changed, continuing through the 1970s and 1980s to the end of the Cold War.

Enough Should Have Been Enough

In its quest to deter the Soviet Union from attacking the United States with nuclear weapons, the United States con-sistently maintained an excessively large nuclear arsenal, and it was often to blame for nuclear innovations that escalated the arms race. Of course, the United States was the first to use the atom bomb. It was also the first to develop the hydrogen bomb (a thousand times more powerful than the atom bomb), submarine-launched ballistic missiles (SLBMs), missiles with multiple warheads, and nuclear-tipped cruise missiles.

The United States also allowed the quantitative arms race to spiral out of control. In the 1950s Eisenhower ordered the production of thousands of nuclear weapons and hundreds of strategic bombers. Kennedy developed hundreds of SLBMs and more than a thousand land-based missiles, called intercontinental-range ballistic missiles.

The first nuclear arms–control treaty, the Strategic Arms Limitation Talks (SALT I), supposedly put a cap on offensive weapons. Yet under Richard Nixon, Jimmy Carter and Ronald Reagan, America's nuclear arsenal kept growing, from about four thousand weapons capable of striking Soviet territory from afar in 1972, when SALT I was signed, to ten thousand

The nuclear arms buildup in the United States continued unabated under President John F. Kennedy.

by the end of Carter's term in office. (And this does not even count thousands of shorter-range missiles!)

Deterrence was based on the theory of mutual assured destruction (MAD): If each superpower had a nuclear arsenal capable of destroying the other superpower, both would be deterred from waging nuclear war. Yet both superpowers had enough nuclear weapons to destroy the planet many times over, far more than what was needed for MAD. Additionally, many scientists believed that a major nuclear war could have put millions of tons of dirt and debris in the atmosphere, creating an Earth-swaddling cloud that would block out sunlight, sending the planet into a deep freeze. Such a nuclear winter would last long enough to end most life on Earth since plants would not be able to grow, causing animals up and down the food chain to perish from starvation.

Pointless Policies

The obscenely large nuclear arsenals were bad enough. Incredibly, the U.S. military under Carter and Reagan also spent enormous amounts of time and money making elaborate plans for prolonged nuclear war. Conservatives claimed that the Soviets believed they could fight and win a nuclear war. But as Soviet specialist Marshall Shulman notes, the USSR's political and military leaders showed "unequivocal awareness that nuclear war would be a danger to the security of their country."[3]

American planning for protracted nuclear war was not only pointless but dangerous as well. American plans included options for nuclear strikes against Soviet nuclear weapons and against Soviet leaders themselves, which, to Moscow, looked like an effort to attain a war-winning capability. In reality, such fears (on both sides) were groundless. In a world of thousands of nuclear weapons, it was foolish to think that either side could hope to fight and win a nuclear war. But the reality was less important than the Soviets' perception of it. America's huge nuclear arsenal only forced the insecure Soviets to build more nuclear weapons and to put their weapons on a hair trigger out of fear that they would have no choice but to use them or lose them.

The Nuclear Peace: Sound Policy or Dumb Luck?

Defenders of U.S. nuclear policy claim that deterrence and U.S. strength kept the nuclear peace during the Cold War. The evidence for this claim is flimsy. Obviously the nuclear peace held, but the test period was less than a half-century long, a mere moment in historical time. Additionally, the Soviets probably never intended to attack the United States with nuclear weapons, so perhaps there was nothing to deter.

A better case could be made for the argument that only dumb luck kept the superpowers from blundering into disaster. Several crises produced dangerously close calls. In the 1962 Cuban missile crisis, for example, President Kennedy thought there was almost a fifty-fifty chance of nuclear war, and each time that his defense secretary went to the White House during the crisis, he feared he would never see his family again.

There were numerous false alarms—atmospheric conditions, defective computer chips, and even flocks of geese creating radar blips that U.S. military officials mistook for incoming Soviet missiles—that could have produced accidental nuclear war. The sheer number of nuclear weapons posed ever-present dangers of unauthorized use and accidents. In one instance, a bomber accidentally released a nuclear bomb over a town in South Carolina (without detonation, fortunately), and in several cases bombers carrying nuclear bombs crashed.

The heavily nuclearized world of the Cold War was indeed MAD. As President Kennedy warned in the 1960s,

> Today, every inhabitant of this planet must contemplate the day when this planet may no longer be habitable. Every man, woman, and child lives under a nuclear sword of Damocles, hanging by the slenderest

of threads, capable of being cut at any moment by accident or miscalculation or by madness. The weapons of war must be abolished before they abolish us.[4]

Sadly, even in the post–Cold War world, this vision of nuclear disarmament has still not been realized.

1. Bernard Brodie, *The Absolute Weapon*. New York: Harcourt, Brace, 1946, p. 76.

2. Quoted in John B. Harris and Eric Markusen, eds., *Nuclear Weapons and the Threat of Nuclear War*. New York: Harcourt Brace Jovanovich, 1986, p. 190.

3. Marshall D. Shulman, "What the Russians Really Want: A Rational Response to the Soviet Nuclear Challenge," *Harper's Magazine*, April 1984, p. 68.

4. Quoted in Charles W. Kegley Jr. and Eugene R. Wittkopf, *American Foreign Policy: Pattern and Process*. New York: St. Martin's, 1996, p. 109.

"The United States had no choice but to meet the Soviet nuclear threat."

U.S. Nuclear Policies Were Necessary and Responsible

The advent of the nuclear era brought challenges and responsibilities for the United States. Critics could cringe at the dreadfulness of nuclear weapons, and they could wish that nuclear weapons would simply go away. Policymakers, on the other hand, had to deal with the real world and the reality of nuclear weapons. During the Cold War, the real world was also one in which an undemocratic, expansionist state possessed an expanding arsenal of nuclear weapons aimed at the United States and its allies.

Nuclear Weapons in U.S. Strategy

Throughout the Cold War, U.S. presidents had to rely on nuclear weapons for extended deterrence—that is, the prevention of attacks against America's closest allies. Extended deterrence was especially important for the defense of Western Europe. The independence and security of Western Europe was vitally important to the United States, but Europe was hard to defend. The Soviet Union had a massive land army and was situated close to America's European allies. In particular, Soviet combat aircraft could reach West Germany—Western Europe's pivotal country—in about five minutes.

45

The United States, on the other hand, is separated from Western Europe by three thousand miles of ocean. Because Western Europe is comparatively small, there was a great danger that much of Europe could be overrun before the North Atlantic Treaty Organization (NATO) could mount serious resistance. The danger was acute because Soviet forces were heavily armored and thus designed for rapid offensive operations. By the 1980s, the Warsaw Pact fielded more than fifty thousand main battle tanks versus only twenty thousand for NATO. Neither the United States nor any other member of NATO could spend the huge amounts of money that it would have taken to match the Soviets.

Nuclear weapons were not only cheap (compared to conventional forces), but they were also a better deterrent. Soviet leaders were ruthless, but they were not mad. They consistently showed a healthy fear of nuclear conflict. Consequently, U.S. strategy—which threatened to turn a European war into a nuclear war—removed any temptation Moscow might have had to commit aggression against Germany or other NATO members.

Conversely, if the United States and Europe had publicly given up the right to use nuclear weapons first, it would have been much easier for Soviet leaders to calculate the costs and gains of initiating war in Europe. Thus, conventional war would have been much more likely, a prospect that terrified European leaders. Any major war fought in Europe, even without the use of nuclear weapons, would have been catastrophic— probably worse than World War II, which killed 50 million people. As the most effective deterrent to Soviet aggression in Europe, the American nuclear umbrella over Western Europe was the glue that held the NATO alliance together. Without it, the alliance might well have fallen apart. The Europeans might have made their own accommodations with the Russians, creating dangerous uncertainty and instability in Europe.

Nuclear weapons also played an important role in ending crises and containing Communist expansionism in other regions. Harry Truman, Dwight Eisenhower, John F. Kennedy, Richard Nixon, and Jimmy Carter all used nuclear threats—cautiously vague and conditional ones, not dangerous or provocative attempts at nuclear blackmail—to ease and end a number of crises. More generally, the mere existence of nuclear weapons and the professed willingness of the United States to use them to defend foreign policy interests acted to constrain Soviet foreign policy adventurism.

U.S. Nuclear Policy: Sanity in a MAD World

As former British prime minister Winston Churchill asserted, peace in the nuclear age is the sturdy child of a calculated, "delicate balance of terror."[1] Neither superpower could protect itself from nuclear annihilation by the other. If either launched a first strike, the other would have enough surviving nuclear weapons to ensure that the attacker would be devastated by the retaliatory blow. Thus, paradoxically, peace was a product of mutual deterrence, known as mutual assured destruction (MAD).

In the 1960s Americans learned to accept the reality of mutual assured destruction. The Soviets did not. Deeply respectful of human life, Americans believed that the very idea of nuclear war with millions of casualties was virtually unthinkable. Therefore, nuclear war "cannot be won and must never be fought," as President Reagan stated repeatedly. The Soviets, who saw 20 million perish in World War II and who killed many millions more of their own people, had a different attitude about war, including nuclear war. For struggle-hardened Soviet leaders, nuclear war was thinkable, and they upgraded their arsenal accordingly. The sheer size of the Soviet arsenal grew rapidly in 1960s. More alarming, however, were the steady modernizations that came in the 1970s and 1980s.

Modernization brought new, larger missiles capable of carrying ten or more nuclear warheads (called multiple independently targetable reentry vehicles), and the number of warheads increased substantially as these new missiles were developed.

Further, these missiles were highly accurate, creating the danger that the thousands of warheads could be targeted on U.S. ballistic missiles, bombers, and submarines in port as well as U.S. leadership and communication systems.

The Soviets also invested heavily in other weapons systems designed to nullify America's retaliatory forces, such as anti-submarine warfare techniques to hunt out and destroy the twenty U.S. nuclear missile–carrying submarines at sea at any given time. The USSR built the thickest air-defense system in the world—thousands of interceptor fighters and surface-to-air missiles supported by a dense radar network—intended to shoot down U.S. bombers not already destroyed on the ground at home by a missile barrage. The Soviets also spent large sums on civil defenses, including huge underground bunker complexes for the leadership, and on the design and location of industrial facilities in order to minimize the effects of any American retaliatory strikes.

Taken together, all of these measures revealed a dangerous mindset about nuclear weapons, leading Harvard historian Richard Pipes to contend in 1977 that "the Soviet Union thinks it can fight and win a nuclear war."[2] Soviet nuclear measures were also part of a broader military buildup that was both huge and extremely costly. The great burden of military spending on the economy, about 25 percent of the gross national product (in contrast to the U.S. defense burden, which was roughly 6 percent of the gross national product), demonstrated just how determined Soviet leaders were to achieve military superiority. Former U.S. defense secretary Harold Brown described Soviet nuclear policy this way: "When we build, they build. When we cut, they build."[3]

No Choice

The United States had no choice but to meet the Soviet nuclear threat, in order to protect the lives of 250 million Americans. The large size of the nuclear arsenal was not the result of mindless escalation by insensitive American leaders.

Rather, the arms race was driven by the need to ensure that the United States could maintain a survivable deterrent in the face of Moscow's relentless buildup. Modernization of American forces and modification of nuclear doctrine were driven by the need to ensure that, in the midst of a crisis (a war between the Soviet Union and China, for example), no desperate Soviet leader could ever have had reason to believe that the USSR could fight and win a nuclear war or gain from nuclear blackmail.

At the same time, U.S. presidents worked to reduce the likelihood of conflict, pursuing increased cooperation and reduced tensions whenever restrained and responsible Soviet conduct made this possible. U.S. presidents also sought to limit the risks of conflict by working with the Soviets on arms-control measures aimed at limiting and reducing nuclear arsenals.

Nuclear weapons are horrible. But no American president could simply wish them away. The prevention of nuclear war required a robust deterrent capability and constant vigilance against Soviet efforts to attain nuclear superiority. Responsible American policy required that the awesome power of the atom be harnessed for the purpose of defending the freedom and security of American citizens and America's vital interests. U.S. nuclear policy during the Cold War was prudent and responsible—and successful.

1. Quoted in John Newhouse, *War and Peace in the Nuclear Age*. New York: Alfred A. Knopf, 1989, p. 81.

2. Richard Pipes, "Why the Soviet Union Thinks It Can Fight and Win a Nuclear War," *Commentary*, July 1977.

3. Quoted in Herbert M. Levine and Jean Edward Smith, eds., *The Conduct of American Foreign Policy Debated*. New York: McGraw-Hill, 1990, p. 374.

"Vietnam typified the wrongheaded foreign policy known as 'containment': America's forty-year effort to stop the spread of Communism in the Third World."

The U.S. Policy of Global Containment Was Costly and Unnecessary: The Case of Vietnam

The Vietnam War was a fiasco for the United States. In an attempt to prevent a Communist victory in South Vietnam, the United States became entangled with corrupt and unpopular governments in Saigon (South Vietnam's capital) from the early 1950s until the Communist triumph in 1975. For eight years (1965–1973) the United States was directly involved in combat against South Vietnamese Communist guerrillas and regular forces from Communist North Vietnam. The futile and foolish enterprise was immensely costly—fifty-eight thousand American soldiers paid with their lives—and it created deep wounds and divisions in American society. Though unique in its duration and costs, U.S. involvement in Vietnam typified the wrongheaded foreign policy known as "containment": America's forty-year effort to stop the spread of Communism in the Third World.

Vietnam: A Strategic Backwater

Vietnam was a poor small country, unimportant to the United States. The question of who controlled South Vietnam had no bearing whatsoever on the global balance of power. Even the U.S. Joint Chiefs of Staff acknowledged this, saying in 1954, "From the point of view of the United States, Indochina is devoid of decisive military objectives and the allocation of more than token U.S. armed forces to that area would be a serious diversion of limited U.S. capabilities."[1]

American Prestige and Credibility

Supporters of U.S. intervention argued that American prestige and the credibility of America's commitments to the North Atlantic Treaty Organization and other allies would suffer if the United States failed to defeat Communism in South Vietnam. But neither would have been called into question if U.S. leaders had chosen not to enter into an unwinnable civil war in a country of no strategic importance to the United States. In fact, the biggest danger to American credibility associated with Vietnam came from the actual intervention, which squandered precious military resources on a hopeless cause.

The Domino Theory Was Wrong

In 1954 President Eisenhower used the metaphor of falling dominoes to justify U.S. support for the government in Saigon. Comparing the countries of Southeast Asia to dominoes, Eisenhower warned, "You knock over the first one, and what will happen to the last one is the certainty that it will go over very quickly."[2] Thus, claimed Eisenhower, South Vietnam's fate was important to the United States.

Other presidents also referred to falling dominoes or some equivalent image to justify Vietnam policy as well as commitments to other strategically unimportant developing countries. But the mechanical image of states falling to Communism, one after another, was a gross oversimplification. As foreign-policy expert James C. Thomson Jr. asserts, the domino theory resulted from "profound ignorance of Asian history and hence ignorance of the radical differences among Asian nations and societies" and from a "blindness to the power and resilience of Asian nationalism."[3] Every country was different, and only a few were vulnerable to Communist insurgencies or pressures from neighbors. When Communist victories did occur, the governments of nearby states redoubled their efforts to strengthen themselves against Communist aggression by increasing their defensive capabilities or by associating themselves with the United States or other non-Communist nations.

Nationalism

American policymakers insisted that the danger in South Vietnam was a Communist victory. They insisted on seeing North Vietnamese leader Ho Chi Minh as a loyal Communist and pawn of the Chinese and Soviets. But the North Vietnamese and their guerrilla allies in the south were nationalists first and Communists only second. The Vietnamese Communist Party was created in 1930 in opposition to French colonialism, and it was sustained by the struggle against Japanese invaders during World War II and against the French when they returned after the war. After 1954 Ho led the struggle to evict the Americans, whom he believed to be the successors to the French colonialists, and to reunify the divided nation.

"Vietnam for the Vietnamese" was the battle cry of Ho's Communists, who were continuing the long struggle for Vietnamese independence. They were not fighting for that independence only to surrender it and become puppets for the Soviets or the Chinese. Moreover, a long history of Chinese domination of Vietnam left a deep reservoir of Vietnamese suspicion and hostility toward the Chinese. Consequently, Americans should have recognized that a Communist triumph in Vietnam would not have strengthened international Communism.

A Civil War, Not Communist Aggression

The U.S. State Department repeatedly referred to North Vietnamese "aggression" across the border between North

and South Vietnam. But this was not a case of aggression. The line of division at the seventeenth parallel was created at the 1954 Geneva Conference on Vietnam as a "provisional" military demarcation line, which "should not in any way be interpreted as constituting a political or territorial boundary,"[4] according to the final declaration of the conference. Thus, the conflict was really a civil war. The distinction was important for two reasons. First, as a matter of international law, aggression against a sovereign nation threatens international peace and security and is therefore much more important to the international community than civil war is. Neither the UN Charter nor any regional treaty required the United States to come to the aid of Saigon in the case of civil war.

Second, part of the military and political failure of the U.S. effort in Vietnam stemmed from faulty analysis of the nature of the conflict. By treating the conflict as one of aggressor versus victim, the United States underestimated the difficulties of fighting a guerrilla conflict. In conventional state-versus-state warfare, it is generally easy to distinguish between friend and foe, combatant and noncombatant. In Vietnam, it was not. In conventional warfare, victory usually goes to the side with bigger guns. In guerrilla warfare, heavy weapons and firepower do not readily translate into victory. Success in guerrilla warfare depends on winning the allegiance and cooperation of the ordinary peasant, but the United States could not do this with a firepower-heavy military strategy that wantonly destroyed villages and farms. The United States could not beat the Communists in a race to win the hearts and minds of Vietnamese peasants because U.S. policy was harnessed to the unpopular South Vietnamese government. As Eric M. Bergerud claims, the regime in South Vietnam was riddled with "inefficiency and wholesale corruption"[5] at every level.

The Bigger Picture: The Folly of U.S. Commitments in the Third World

Vietnam was a tragic, unnecessary, and unwinnable war, and it was unique in its costs to American society. But it was just one of many American commitments in the Third World throughout the Cold War (such as the Korean War of the 1950s and U.S. involvement in Central America in the 1980s). These commitments, however, were unnecessary: a) most Third World countries were not vulnerable to Communist-sponsored insurgencies or revolutions; b) even where successful, Communist governments in the Third World would not take orders from Moscow but did become costly burdens to the Soviet Union; and c) most developing countries were strategically unimportant to the United States in the first place.

Not only was global containment unnecessary, it was very costly and risky for the United States. Containment required an expensive worldwide system of military bases and excessive defense expenditures to defend far-flung commitments. U.S. commitments to developing countries gave many of them a license to raid the U.S. treasury for economic and military aid. As the distinguished journalist Walter Lippmann observed in 1947, "A weak ally is not an asset. It is a liability. It requires the diversion of power, money, and prestige to support it and maintain it."[6] By the 1980s the United States suffered from a condition that the eminent historian Paul Kennedy labeled imperial overstretch. Costly global commitments threatened the nation's economic future; the United States risked being eclipsed in trade and other vital economic areas by Japan and Germany, countries that had no global commitments and spent little on defense.

Global containment also tarnished the moral reputation of the United States because Washington often felt compelled to support governments that were non-Communist but nevertheless brutal and corrupt dictatorships. Containment in the Third World damaged relations with the Soviet Union and China and threatened to turn relatively insignificant conflicts into nuclear powder kegs. Finally, America's obsessive efforts to enforce containment the world over created innumerable potential Vietnam-like quagmires.

1. Quoted in Edwin P. Hoyt, *America's Wars and Military Encounters from Colonial Times to the Present*. New York: Da Capo, 1988, p. 464.

2. Quoted in Thomas G. Paterson and Dennis Merrill, eds., *Major Problems in American Foreign Relations: Documents and Essays*, 4th ed. Lexington, MA: D.C. Heath, 1995, p. 536.

3. Quoted in Charles C. Kegley Jr. and Eugene R. Wittkopf, eds., *Perspectives on American Foreign Policy*. New York: St. Martin's, 1983, p. 380.

4. Quoted in Guenter Lewy, *America in Vietnam*. Oxford, England: Oxford University Press, 1978, p. 8.

5. Quoted in Paterson and Merrill, *Major Problems in American Foreign Relations*, p. 575.

6. Walter Lippmann, "The Cold War," *Foreign Affairs*, Spring 1987, p, 875.

"It would have been foolish and irresponsible for the United States to withdraw altogether from Asia, Africa, and Latin America while allowing the Communist powers free reign in those vast regions."

The U.S. Policy of Global Containment Was Effective: The Case of Vietnam

In the early 1960s South Vietnam, and perhaps much of the rest of Southeast Asia as well, faced a deadly threat from North Vietnam and its Chinese and Soviet backers, who were bent on expanding the sphere of Communist tyranny. If the United States had stood by and done nothing, the Soviets would have gained another small piece on the global chessboard, and the Soviets and the Chinese would have been tempted to probe farther. Even though American intervention in Vietnam ultimately failed, it was nonetheless a "noble cause,"[1] as President Ronald Reagan later called it.

The Moral Issue

The main reason for American intervention in Vietnam was the desire to save the population of South Vietnam from Communist oppression. U.S. officials were entirely correct in believing that however bad the Saigon government was, the Communists were much worse.

When the Communists came to power in North Vietnam in the 1950s, thousands of Vietnamese Catholics fled to the non-Communist south to avoid religious persecution, and tens of thousands more were jailed, tortured, and executed by the dictatorial Communist government.

Developments after the Communist victories in April 1975 confirmed the worst American fears. Tens of thousands of South Vietnamese were sent to so-called reeducation camps for abusive indoctrination in Communist ideology. Hundreds of thousands of courageous but poorly supplied boat people desperately attempted to escape Communist oppression, fleeing in ramshackle boats that were constantly vulnerable to murderous pirates on the South China Sea. Half of them perished.

As bad as things were in Vietnam, they were even worse in neighboring Cambodia when the Communist Khmer Rouge came to power, also in April 1975. The paranoid and fanatically anti-intellectual Khmer Rouge mounted a fierce campaign of terror, putting ordinary people to death, often in gruesome ways, for such "crimes" as possessing books or wearing eyeglasses. Of a population of 7 million, 1 to 2 million died in Cambodia's ghastly killing fields.

Aggression Versus Civil War

Critics of U.S. policy wrongly dismissed the Communists' struggle for power as a mere civil war and asserted that South Vietnamese Communists were independent of North Vietnam. In reality there was only one Communist Party of Vietnam, and it was dominated by North Vietnam. Communists in North Vietnam initiated and directed the fighting and conducted most of the military operations, especially from 1968 on.

North and South Vietnam were effectively two separate countries by 1965 when North Vietnam began large-scale deployments of its regular forces into South Vietnam. The real issue was not about the precise legal status of the border between North and South Vietnam. Instead, the key issue was the fate of the South Vietnamese people, the vast majority of whom had no desire to be forcibly incorporated into a unified Communist Vietnam.

Vietnam, American Strategic Interests, and Falling Dominoes

Critics dismissed the domino theory, but in fact, there were domino-type dangers in the early 1960s when the international climate was favorable to the contagion of Communism. Much of the developing world was liberating itself from European colonialism and was sympathetic to the anti-Western agendas of China and the Soviet Union and to their socialist and anti-democratic systems, which boasted enormous economic and military strides and iron-fisted political stability.

The Soviet Union and China both actively supported revolution and subversion around the globe and poured billions of dollars worth of military aid into North Vietnam. China, which developed nuclear weapons in 1964, was especially threatening because it bordered North Vietnam and espoused a militantly expansionist and bitterly anti-Western version of Communism. For good reason, President John F. Kennedy warned, "China is so large, looms so high just beyond the frontiers, that if South Vietnam went, it would not only give them an improved geographic position for a guerrilla assault on Malaya, but would also give the impression that the wave of the future in southeast Asia was with China and the Communists."[2] Indonesia, the largest nation in Southeast Asia, was already under the control of a pro-Communist government.

As Kennedy's statement suggests, Communist victories provided apparent confirmation for Marxist predictions about the inevitability of Communism, inspiring and energizing revolutionaries while demoralizing non-Communists. Each Communist victory created safe havens and military sanctuaries for nearby revolutionaries and became a source of weaponry to be used against other non-Communist governments.

Vietnam's location facilitated Communist efforts to exert pressure on Laos, Cambodia, Thailand, Burma, and the large island nations of Southeast Asia. It also allowed for the construction of air and naval bases on the South China Sea—bases that were immediately developed and put to use by the Soviet Union after the Communists' victory in 1975.

Critics may have ridiculed the domino theory, but dominoes did fall after the 1975 Communist victory in Vietnam. Cambodia and Laos were taken over by Communists, and more nations might have fallen if not for the rivalry between China and the USSR that developed during the 1960s.

Vietnam and American Resolve, Prestige, and Credibility

Passive American acceptance of a Communist victory in South Vietnam would have damaged American prestige and the world's belief in American resolve. The stakes were high. As President Lyndon Johnson stated, "Around the globe, from Berlin to Thailand, are people whose well-being rests in part on the belief that they can count on us if they are attacked. To leave Vietnam to its fate would shake the confidence of all these people in the value of an American commitment and in the value of America's word."[3]

In the dangerous world of the 1960s, American retreat and defeat in Vietnam would have left U.S. friends and allies less willing to defy the Communist superpowers or to resist their attempts at global expansionism. By the same token, the Communist powers would have been emboldened to test the United States if American resolve had faltered in Southeast Asia. In Korea, Berlin, Cuba, and elsewhere, China and the Soviet Union often probed and tested the United States. Thus, as President Johnson declared, "The central lesson of our time is that the appetite of aggression is never satisfied. To withdraw from one battlefield means only to prepare for the next. We must say in Southeast Asia—as we did in Europe—in the words of the Bible: 'Hitherto shalt thou come, but no further.'"[4]

South Vietnam was not vitally important to the United States, but that does not mean that it was entirely unimportant. No president could watch passively as it was swallowed by Communist North Vietnam. The stability of Southeast Asia and the credibility of American commitments were at

Marines look for North Vietnamese army bunkers during the Tet offensive, the 1968 Communist attack on nearly every major city and province in South Vietnam.

stake. Nor could the United States be true to its own ideals if it failed to help people threatened by aggressive efforts to widen the sphere of Communist tyranny. The war was costly to the United States, and critics are correct in asserting that the U.S. war effort up to 1968 suffered from serious flaws. But they were wrong to conclude that the war was unwinnable. The Communists suffered a crushing defeat in their massive offensive of 1968 (the Tet offensive), and U.S. military strategy became much sounder from then on. Unfortunately, the success of antiwar protesters led to rapid American disengagement and defunding of the war effort. America's final withdrawal from Vietnam in 1975 was a tragedy for our South Vietnamese allies whose soldiers and citizens were abandoned to be brutalized by Communist tyrants.

Communist Expansionism in the Third World

Frustrated by their inability to expand into Europe and other industrialized regions, the Communist powers focused on opportunities in the developing world. A secret Chinese Communist Party document in 1963 called developing countries "the most vulnerable areas under imperialist rule, and the storm-centers of world revolution."[5] Chinese leader Mao Tse-tung declared that conflicts in the Third World would "prove decisive in the current phase of world revolution."[6] The Chinese took guerrilla war strategy as a model for global Communist victory: Seize the countryside (the developing world) first, and then strangle the cities (the industrialized world). In the later stages of the Cold War, the Soviet Union, buttressed by its enormous military buildup, posed the greatest threat to global peace and security because of its expansionist efforts in the Third World.

The Communist giants clearly recognized the strategic importance of the Third World. Rapidly growing developing countries comprised a majority of Earth's population. Much of the world's strategic minerals and other resources, including oil, were located in developing countries, as were the fastest growing economies. Many developing countries came to acquire impressive modernized armies. And, developing countries fronted most of the waterways that were the avenues of commerce and naval operations for the United States and the rest of the world. By the late 1980s the USSR was using military facilities in Angola, Cuba, Ethiopia, South Yemen, Syria, and Vietnam that could have played a "decisive role in the event of a major war between the United States and the Soviet Union,"[7] as foreign policy researcher Steven R. David argues.

It would have been foolish and irresponsible for the United States to withdraw altogether from Asia, Africa, and Latin America while allowing the Communist powers free reign in those vast regions. Fortunately, American presidents wisely followed the sage advice offered by Sovietologist George Kennan in 1947, pursuing the "adroit and vigilant application of counterforce at a series of constantly shifting geographical and political points."[8] The policy of global containment, pursued patiently, firmly, and responsibly by the United States, maintained global peace and security for forty-five years, until the virus of Soviet-style Communism finally died a natural death.

1. Quoted in Andrew J. Rotter, ed., *Light at the End of the Tunnel: A Vietnam War Anthology.* New York: St. Martin's, 1991, p. 433.

2. Quoted in Rotter, *Light at the End of the Tunnel*, p. 127.

3. Quoted in Bruce W. Jentleson, "American Commitments in the Third World: Theory vs. Practice," *International Organization*, Autumn 1987, p. 676.

4. Quoted in Thomas G. Paterson and Dennis Merrill, eds., *Major Problems in American Foreign Relations: Documents and Essays*, 4th ed. Lexington, MA: D.C. Heath, 1995, p. 541.

5. Quoted in R.B. Smith, *An International History of the Vietnam War*, Vol. 2, *The Struggle for Southeast Asia, 1961–65.* New York: St. Martin's, 1985, p. 77.

6. Quoted in Smith, *An International History of the Vietnam War*, p. 87.

7. Steven R. David, "Why the Third World Matters," *International Security*, Summer 1989, p. 65.

8. Mr. X (George Kennan), "The Sources of Soviet Conduct," *Foreign Affairs*, Spring 1987, p. 862.

*"Because of confrontational policies inspired by hawkish
enemies of détente, the United States failed to grasp a
major opportunity."*

The Policy of Détente Failed Because of American Chauvinism

U.S.-Soviet relations entered their most promising phase at the
start of the 1970s. President Richard Nixon and Soviet leader
Leonid Brezhnev held two summit conferences and concluded
a number of treaties and other agreements in what came to be
called the period of détente, the French term for the relaxation
of tensions. The quarter-century long Cold War appeared to be
over. Yet within a few short years, détente was but a fond mem-
ory as the superpowers lapsed into another phase of dangerously competitive relations. Because of confrontational
American policies inspired by hawkish enemies of détente, the
United States failed to grasp a major opportunity. It wasn't the
first time. Throughout the Cold War, U.S. policymakers
allowed opportunities for improved relations to slip away.

A Pattern of Missed Opportunities

From President Harry Truman on, American presidents suc-
cumbed to exaggerated fears of the Soviet threat and to political
pressures from domestic anti-Communist forces. In the early
1950s the hysteria of McCarthyism—the anti-Communist witch
hunt initiated by Wisconsin senator Joseph McCarthy—made

any accommodation with Communist countries seem like treason. President Dwight Eisenhower's Soviet policy was largely shaped by his rigidly anti-Communist secretary of state, John Foster Dulles. Dulles refused to accept that the death of Soviet dictator Joseph Stalin in 1953 might improve U.S.-Soviet relations. Dulles persuaded Eisenhower to act cautiously in a 1955 summit conference with the new Soviet leaders, even though the Soviets had made important concessions on several issues. At the end of the Eisenhower presidency another promising opening in U.S.-Soviet relations was squandered when an American U-2 spy plane was shot down over Soviet territory in May 1960, ruining an East-West summit conference in Paris.

President John F. Kennedy's administration started badly when the United States sponsored a futile invasion of Cuba,

A medium-range ballistic missile base in Cuba. The Cuban missile crisis of 1962 nearly ignited a nuclear war between the United States and the Soviet Union.

Moscow's only ally in the Caribbean, at the Bay of Pigs. A promising thaw followed the 1962 Cuban missile crisis as the superpowers agreed to establish a crisis hot line and to ban atmospheric nuclear tests. Unfortunately, this was shortly followed by America's disastrous intervention in Vietnam, and another opportunity was lost.

President Lyndon Johnson could have undertaken negotiations with the Soviets to limit nuclear arms, but the president's preoccupation with Vietnam and his overreaction to Moscow's 1968 intervention in Czechoslovakia, which was aimed at ending an experiment in reform Communism in that Warsaw Pact nation, eliminated yet another chance to ease Cold War tensions.

The Détente Opportunity

At no time were the chances for ending the Cold War better than at the start of the 1970s. The Soviets had caught up to the United States in the nuclear arms race, fostering Soviet confidence and creating a real opportunity for mutual nuclear arms control. Deep tensions between the USSR and China culminated in armed clashes along their shared border. Worried about war with China, the Soviets had an unmistakable interest in reaching accommodation with Europe and the United States. In Europe, the Soviet Union and its Warsaw Pact allies at long last signed peace treaties with Germany. And, in the economic sphere, the Soviet Union was finally abandoning autarchy (nearly complete national self-reliance) in favor of economic engagement with the Western world.

Tensions and the ever-present danger of war were the defining features of the Cold War. By the end of the 1960s, though, the Soviets understood that war between the superpowers would be suicidal in a world marked by huge nuclear arsenals. They clearly had no desire for war. Even U.S. secretary of state Henry A. Kissinger acknowledged that Soviet leader Leonid Brezhnev was expressing a genuine desire for peace when he "spoke often, and on occasion movingly, about the suffering and trauma of the Second World War,"[1] in which 20 million Soviet citizens died.

Under the favorable international circumstances of the détente period, the opportunities for reduced tensions and improved relations between the superpowers were great. In 1969 the Soviets agreed to begin negotiations to limit nuclear arms. The negotiations, called the Strategic Arms Limitation Talks (SALT), produced two SALT treaties in 1972: the first ever break in the nuclear arms race. Negotiations immediately commenced for the next SALT accord.

Washington and Moscow also signed an Agreement for the Prevention of Nuclear War. The Soviets signed an agreement guaranteeing Western access to West Berlin, the earlier focal point of two of the Cold War's most dangerous crises. The Soviets also agreed to negotiations on reducing armored forces in Europe, and they participated in talks aimed at improving security and human rights throughout Europe. Many in the West thought the Cold War would soon be over, and some agreed with Soviet leader Brezhnev, who proclaimed that the Cold War had ended.

Opportunity Squandered: Détente Goes Sour

Despite détente's achievements and potential, the Nixon administration and right-wing, anti-Soviet critics demanded too much of the Soviet Union. The danger of aggression or surprise attack by the Soviets against the West had almost completely vanished, but American hard-liners were not satisfied. They apparently expected the Soviets to stop competing with the United States altogether and to cease being Communists. But as Harvard scholar Stanley Hoffmann notes, the Soviets had "no intention of giving up ideological conflict"[2] with the West, and they certainly did not see détente as requiring them to stop supporting Communist or pro-Soviet forces worldwide.

The Nixon administration and congressional hawks reacted hysterically when the Soviets supported North Vietnam in its war against American and South Vietnamese forces and when Moscow provided military aid to Arab states that went to war against Israel in 1973. But what were the Soviets to do—simply abandon their friends in the name of good relations with the United States? In fact, in the months leading up to the 1973 war in Israel (the Yom Kippur War), Soviet leaders tried desperately to alert U.S. officials to the growing danger of war in the Middle East—clear proof that the Soviets did not instigate the war—but Nixon officials failed to act and then unfairly blamed the Soviets for the conflict.

A Return to the Politics of Confrontation

After the Yom Kippur War superpower relations deteriorated rapidly. The Soviets never saw the fruits of the 1972 U.S.-Soviet trade agreement because the U.S. Congress demanded that the Soviets agree (in writing!) to meet U.S.-specified targets for increased Jewish emigration from the USSR in return for expanded trade. This linking of two completely unrelated issues was humiliating to the proud Russians. Unsurprisingly, the Soviets angrily refused to jump through congressional hoops to expand trade that would benefit both countries. As Soviet affairs expert Raymond L. Garthoff concludes, the Soviet government, "with considerable justification, considered itself the victim of double-dealing or incompetence by the American administration,"[3] which failed to resist action by Congress.

After Nixon, America's Soviet policy was effectively hijacked or held hostage by anti-Communist ideologues. In the year leading up to the 1976 presidential election, Republican president Gerald Ford was under such intense pressure from his party's right wing that he ordered administration officials to ban the word détente from their public pronouncements. Private groups of defense intellectuals conducted a shrill but effective campaign against arms control based on grossly exaggerated estimates of Soviet strategic nuclear capabilities and on unfounded charges about Soviet cheating on SALT I.

The Soviets were blamed for causing turbulence in the Third World while the real causes—poverty and injustice (both frequently worsened by U.S.-backed right-wing dictatorships)—were conveniently ignored by the U.S. government. The importance of the Third World was exaggerated, as was the extent of Soviet gains.

Democratic president Jimmy Carter, under intense pressure from conservative Republicans, also opted for confrontation over détente. The Carter administration subjected the Soviets to embarrassing public criticisms over human rights, leading the authors of one text on American foreign policy to conclude that "Carter's call for human rights counted as yet another example of Washington's abandonment of detente."[4] Carter pushed NATO into endorsing both conventional and nuclear modernization programs. Recklessly, the Carter administration forged a strategic partnership with the USSR's worst enemy, China. The American president also reacted hysterically when the Soviets intervened in Afghanistan in December 1979, calling the "invasion" the "greatest threat to peace since the Second World War,"[5] and claiming that the Soviets were motivated by a desire to take over the Persian Gulf. Carter ignored that the Soviets acted only very reluctantly in this poor, small, strategically unimportant country and that their intervention was aimed at saving a Marxist-Leninist government that was in danger of being overthrown by fanatical Muslim rebels. Tensions rose to 1950s' levels as the United States imposed a grain embargo on the USSR, boycotted the 1980 Moscow Olympics, and initiated several provocative military programs.

The election of the militantly anti-Communist Ronald Reagan in 1980 was the final nail in the coffin of détente. Reagan's bitterly anti-Soviet rhetoric and his wasteful and dangerous military policies consistently insulted and threatened the Soviets. Only the selection of the courageous and far-sighted Mikhail Gorbachev as Soviet leader in 1985 rescued the superpower relationship from a seemingly endless deep freeze of confrontation.

A Sad Record of Policy Failure

Throughout the Cold War, American presidents repeatedly missed opportunities to ease tensions and improve relations with the USSR. Presidents Ford, Carter, and Reagan missed the biggest opportunities. During their presidencies, détente was ruined by unrealistic expectations and exaggerated views of the Soviet threat. Rather than seizing opportunities to end the Cold War, post-détente presidents pandered to right-wing anti-Communist pressures, pursuing risky and counterproductive policies of confrontation.

1. Henry A. Kissinger, *White House Years*. Boston: Little, Brown, 1979, p. 1,143.

2. Quoted in Joseph S. Nye Jr., ed., *The Making of America's Soviet Policy*. New Haven, CT: Yale University Press, 1984, p. 243.

3. Raymond L. Garthoff, *Détente and Confrontation: American-Soviet Relations from Nixon to Reagan*. Washington, DC: Brookings, 1985, p. 460.

4. Thomas G. Paterson, J. Garry Clifford, and Kenneth J. Hagan, *American Foreign Relations: A History*, 4th ed. Lexington, MA: D.C. Heath, 1995, p. 501.

5. Quoted in Bernard A. Weisberger, *Cold War, Cold Peace: The United States and Russia Since 1945*. Boston: Houghton Mifflin, 1984, p. 291.

"If the movement from Cold War to detente is progress, then . . . [the United States] cannot afford more such progress."

The Policy of Détente Failed Because of Soviet Aggressiveness

The West deluded itself at the start of the 1970s when it believed that the Soviet Union had changed and that the Cold War might be over. Contrary to wishful thinking in Europe and the United States, the Soviet Union was as hostile and as expansionist as ever. At worst, the Soviets even used détente as a weapon to deceive and disarm the West while the USSR pursued its quest for global domination.

Nixon Gives Détente a Chance

President Richard Nixon first gave détente a chance. In the name of peace, he began comprehensive negotiations with the Russians in 1969, even though Soviet tanks had brutally crushed Czechoslovakia's experiment with a more humane reform socialism just a year earlier. He traveled to Moscow for a summit conference in May 1972, even though Soviet-backed North Vietnamese forces had launched a major offensive against American and South Vietnamese soldiers just weeks earlier. He signed a Basic Principles Agreement with the Soviets, which laid out the basic ground rules for U.S.-Soviet relations, even though he had reason to believe (correctly as it turned out) that

71

the Soviets would not abide by the agreement's terms. He signed two Strategic Arms Limitation Talks (SALT) agreements, even though he could anticipate cheating and efforts to gain nuclear superiority by the Soviets. And he signed a U.S.-Soviet trade pact that was highly favorable to the Russians.

In spite of an improved atmosphere and the signing of numerous accords, détente did not bring durable changes in Soviet behavior, and the easing of tensions was only temporary. The Soviet leopard had not changed its spots and was, in fact, becoming more dangerous as it became more powerful. In the years following détente's 1972 high point, Soviet behavior failed to improve, and in some cases, it became worse.

Soviet Domination of Eastern Europe

Several of the agreements concluded under détente required the Soviet Union to relax its grip over Eastern Europe. Unfortunately, this did not happen and life did not improve very much for Eastern Europeans. The most conspicuous symbol of tyranny, the Berlin Wall, remained in place, and the Communist East German government continued to shoot those who attempted to flee to freedom. Moscow continued to be the final authority for both foreign and domestic policies in Eastern Europe.

In Poland, the Soviets looked on threateningly as Solidarity, the first independent trade union ever to emerge in a Communist country, grew rapidly in the late 1970s to defend workers' rights and challenge the authority of the Communist Party. In December 1981, under heavy pressure from Moscow, the Polish government outlawed this immensely popular union and declared martial law. Détente and détente-era agreements prohibiting such repressive behavior utterly failed to bring freedom to Eastern Europe. Détente failed in large part because of Moscow's cynical and brutal suppression of Solidarity.

Soviet Pressures on Western Europe

While using an iron fist to maintain uniformity and Soviet control in Eastern Europe, the Soviets did not hesitate to use détente to foster divisions within the North Atlantic Treaty Organization (NATO) alliance. They also used threats and military power to intimidate Western Europe.

Throughout the 1970s the Soviets worked to undermine NATO's cohesion. As Americans became disillusioned with détente, the Soviets dangled export opportunities in front of Western Europeans to keep them wedded to détente no matter how badly the Soviets behaved. The Soviets were particularly effective in using their control over access routes to West Berlin and over human contacts across divided Germany to keep the West Germans unconditionally committed to a détente relationship.

In the talks over conventional forces in Europe, the Soviets stubbornly refused to make any concessions that would reduce their threatening superiority in armored forces. The talks proved to be a sham, grinding on for almost two decades without results.

Although the Soviets already had two types of intermediate-range missiles targeted on Western Europe while NATO had no intermediate-range missiles targeted on the Soviet Union, the Soviets began deploying new nuclear forces directed against Western Europe: a medium-range bomber called the Backfire, and a highly accurate three-warhead missile called the SS-20. Deploying SS-20s at the rate of one a week, the Soviets soon had several hundred aimed at European targets. The Soviets subjected the Europeans to strong pressures, occasionally punctuated by threats, to discourage them from responding to the USSR's nuclear deployments.

The Soviets did not want war in Europe. But they did want to shape European foreign and defense policies through fear, creating a dark, frightening shadow of military power. Détente did nothing to improve this unsettling situation.

Soviet Military Power

In the 1970s the Soviets engaged in a far-reaching expansion and modernization of military forces. Despite its backbreaking costs, this immense buildup was undertaken even as the

United States was moving in precisely the opposite direction, reducing its global military presence and commitments and cutting its defense budget by about 2 percent per year.

Western Europe was not the only region affected by the Soviet buildup. The United States was threatened by the USSR's ambitious expansion and modernization of strategic nuclear forces, which threatened to enable the Soviet Union to fight and win a nuclear war. The Soviets also threatened global peace and security through the development of a so-called blue-water navy (that is, one capable of operating throughout the oceans of the world) and greater power projection capabilities. As Soviet expert Vernon V. Aspaturian notes, this meant that the Soviet Union was no longer merely a superpower but had become a "global power"[1] as well. Thus, during the détente era, the military threat from the USSR increased substantially.

Soviet Activism in the Third World

The Soviet Union's military buildup helped to expand its influence in the Third World. In turn, the USSR's gains in particular Third World countries provided the Soviets with bases and facilities that allowed them to further expand their global influence. Using large-scale weapons transfers, paramilitary support for Communist dictators, and direct military involvement, the Soviets achieved substantial gains in the Third World in the decade following the 1972 Moscow summit. With their Cuban allies, the Soviets intervened directly in several civil and regional conflicts.

Soviet movements in the direction of the Persian Gulf were especially worrisome. A key strategic goal for the Soviets had always been to control the oil-rich Persian Gulf, the West's jugular vein. As regional specialist Shahram Chubin observes, "The frontiers of the Russian state have constantly expanded southward, sometimes glacially, sometimes abruptly."[2] Things occurred abruptly in late 1979, when the Soviet Union invaded Afghanistan, the first ever direct intervention by Soviet forces outside the Warsaw Pact area. Even President Jimmy Carter, the most dovish of the postwar presidents, recognized that the invasion "threatens both Iran and Pakistan and is a steppingstone to possible control over much of the world's oil supplies,"[3] thus constituting a "grave threat to world peace."[4] For eight years the Soviets continued to wage a savage war against the small poor country of Muslim tribespeople.

By the start of the 1980s, the Soviets were even meddling in conflicts in Central America, threatening the stability of a region near the United States itself. The 1972 Basic Principles Agreement had called on both superpowers to exercise self-restraint, but the Soviets flagrantly disregarded their obligation, instead using the era of relaxed tensions to score victories over the United States, threatening the global balance of power in the process.

Human Rights

American hopes that détente would lead to improvements in Soviet human rights practices were also disappointed. The Soviets continued to be intolerant of political opposition. Prominent opponents of the government were arrested and jailed or exiled. Some were forcibly confined in psychiatric institutions, their dissent treated as a form of mental illness. Like other Communist countries, the Soviet Union was a virtual prison for its people; the right to emigrate was highly restricted. Despite their commitments to respect human rights, the Soviets loudly condemned all criticisms of their atrocious human rights record.

The Failure of Détente

Western liberals were deluded in believing that détente meant an end to the Cold War. The American architects of détente can be credited with giving peace a chance. American leaders genuinely wanted accommodation with the Soviet Union in a world order that was peaceful, stable, and secure. The Soviets wanted to be the world's paramount power. They did not want mutual accommodation but rather victory in the Cold War. They used détente and détente-era agreements as part of their broader struggle to win the Cold War. Caspar Weinberger, President Ronald Reagan's secretary of defense, thus had it exactly right when he complained, "If the movement from Cold War to detente is progress, then let me say we cannot afford more such progress."[5]

1. Vernon V. Aspaturian, "Soviet Global Power and the Correlation of Forces," *Problems of Communism*, May/June 1980, p. 1.

2. Shahram Chubin, "U.S. Security Interests in the Persian Gulf in the 1980s," *Daedalus*, Fall 1980, p. 45.

3. *Weekly Compilation of Presidential Documents*, January 14, 1980, p. 26.

4. Quoted in Mark Heller, *The Soviet Invasion of Afghanistan: Motivations and Implications*. Tel Aviv: Center for Strategic Studies, 1980, pp. 13–14.

5. Quoted in Raymond L. Garthoff, *Détente and Confrontation: American-Soviet Relations from Nixon to Reagan*. Washington, DC: Brookings, 1985, p. 1,050.

CHAPTER 3

The End of the Cold War

"[U.S.] strength . . . did lead to negotiations, bargaining chips did produce bargains, and 'hanging tough' did eventually pay off."

U.S. Policies in the 1980s Helped End the Cold War

The United States won the Cold War after pursuing over forty-five years of cautious but firm opposition to Communist ideology and the Soviet state. The vigilant policy of containment pursued by the United States repeatedly closed doors to Soviet expansionism, ultimately causing the Soviet system to collapse from the dead weight of its own fundamental flaws. U.S. Cold War policy culminated in the final decade of the Cold War under Presidents Ronald Reagan and George Bush. The Cold War finally came to an end between 1989 and 1991 because of the intense pressure these two presidents put on Soviet leaders to reform their decrepit Communist regime. At the same time, however, Reagan and Bush were careful to respond to Soviet concerns that economic reforms and arms reductions might weaken the USSR militarily.

The Reagan-Bush Era

Ronald Reagan recognized as clearly as anyone that the Soviet Union was afflicted with serious structural weaknesses. Reagan was entirely correct when he called Communism "a sad, bizarre chapter"[1] in human history, although many liberals who sought improved relations with the Soviet Union disapproved of his blunt phrasing. Just after Reagan left office in 1989, the Communist system imploded, crumbling because of the sharp internal contradictions of Communism. Reagan policies helped accelerate that process.

Ronald Reagan did much to restore American power and confidence. Under his leadership the United States took the lead in promoting two great global trends of the 1980s, one toward democratization and the other toward market-oriented economics over socialism and other statist approaches to economic affairs. Soviet Communism was out of phase with both. Reagan, often called "the Great Communicator," was an eloquent spokesman for American democracy and free markets, which provided models for people the world over. In the international marketplace of ideas, America's stock went way up while the Soviet Union's plummeted.

But Reagan did much more than beat the Soviets in the realm of ideological competition. After a decade of neglect, American military forces were expanded and modernized. The USSR was put on notice that the détente era, marked by numerous Soviet gains in the Third World and elsewhere, was over. The United States would thwart further Soviet advances while prudently applying pressure that would push the USSR in the direction of reform.

The Reagan Doctrine

The Soviet Union had recorded a string of successes in the Third World during the late 1970s while the United States turned inward as a result of the Vietnam War. The Reagan administration recognized that the rise to power of Marxist regimes in Vietnam, Afghanistan, Angola, Mozambique, Benin, South Yemen, and Nicaragua created costly new obligations and vulnerabilities for Moscow. Earlier in the Cold War, China and the Soviet Union had supported Vietnamese Communists, raising costs and denying victory to the United States in Vietnam. Now the United States could turn the tables. In

Angola, Nicaragua, Cambodia, and Afghanistan, U.S.-backed insurgencies challenged Soviet-backed governments.

In Afghanistan, for example, the United States provided military aid to Muslim rebels who were resisting a fierce military campaign conducted by the Soviets. That aid included hand-held Stinger antiaircraft guns that enabled the Afghan freedom fighters to down many attack jets and helicopter gunships, blunting the Soviets' deadly air superiority. Frustrated by the inability to defeat the U.S.-backed rebels, Soviet leader Mikhail Gorbachev complained that the war was a bleeding wound for the Soviet Union and soon negotiated with the United States, reaching a settlement that brought a complete Soviet withdrawal.

Afghanistan was but the most dramatic example of the successful U.S. policy. As John Spanier and Steven W. Hook conclude in their book *American Foreign Policy Since World War II*, the Reagan Doctrine was "a cost-effective means of putting pressure on Moscow, which had to spend an estimated $10–20 billion a year (compared with less than $1 billion annually for the United States) to preserve the gains it had achieved in the 1970s."[2] In the late 1980s Soviet leaders realized that the costs were too great and ended their policy of global adventurism.

The Military-Technological Revolution and SDI

Even more powerful American pressure was exerted in the military arena. Despite the Soviet Union's astronomical military buildup of the 1970s, it could not hope to win an extended arms race with the United States. The Soviet economy could produce massive numbers of tanks and missiles, but it could not produce the miniaturized sensors and guidance systems that allow smart bombs and other precision-guided munitions to dominate the modern battlefield. Reagan's Strategic Defense Initiative (SDI), aimed at developing a system of defenses against nuclear weapons, was a showcase for the military-technological revolution.

Reagan envisioned the SDI as a satellite system that would shoot down nuclear missiles before they could reach their targets. When Reagan first announced plans to build the SDI in 1983, his statement had two profound effects on the Soviet Union. First, it illustrated that Moscow's long-standing goal of attaining strategic nuclear superiority over the United States was futile. Instead, they faced a competition in defensive technologies, which posed insurmountable obstacles of costs and technical challenges. Second, the SDI convinced Gorbachev that a major restructuring, called perestroika, of the Soviet economy was necessary if the Soviet Union were to have any hope of maintaining its status as a superpower over the long haul.

But the social and political forces unleashed in the name of reform created stresses and strains that overwhelmed the brittle Communist system. Ironically then, reforms undertaken to save Soviet Communism ultimately destroyed it, ending the Cold War in the process. Reagan's SDI deserves much of the credit.

The Softer Side of Reagan-Bush Policies

While resisting Soviet expansionism and applying forceful pressures to the Soviet system, Reagan was careful not to provoke the Soviets or back them into a corner. Like earlier presidents, Reagan went to great lengths to reassure the Soviets that the United States was neither aggressive nor a threat to Soviet security. President Reagan was open to negotiations and cooperation with the Soviets. His administration worked hard to reach agreements with the Soviet Union to reduce strategic nuclear arsenals and to eliminate intermediate-range nuclear weapons that posed a deadly threat to Western Europe. Between 1985 and 1988, Reagan held four summit conferences with Mikhail Gorbachev.

Reagan's conciliatory policies gave the Soviets positive incentives for restraint and provided them with the sense of safety that was a necessary precondition for the reform process. Even

U.S. president Ronald Reagan (left) and Soviet leader Mikhail Gorbachev at a 1985 summit meeting in Geneva, Switzerland.

two arch critics of Reagan, Daniel Deudney and G. John Ikenberry, acknowledge that Reagan's "anti-nuclearism" and "intentional engagement"[3] of the Soviet Union were important ingredients in the Cold War's end.

When he took office in 1989, President George Bush continued to engage the Soviets. With great skill, the Bush administration managed the superpower relationship in a period of rapid change, ensuring a soft landing as the Cold War came to a close. As the Soviet empire in Eastern Europe crumbled in the revolutions of 1989 and 1990, President Bush wisely insisted that reunified Germany remain anchored to the West in the North Atlantic Treaty Organization, something that only months earlier Gorbachev had called "unacceptable" and "out of the question."[4] At the same time, however, the American president was "determined not to rub Gorbachev's nose"[5] in Moscow's Eastern European defeats. Instead of gloating, Bush quietly said, "I'm not going to dance on the [Berlin] wall."[6] Bush also offered economic aid and moral support for the reform process in the Soviet Union, and in 1991 he stood resolutely behind Moscow's reformist leaders (Gorbachev and soon-to-be president Boris Yeltsin) when old guard Communists briefly took Gorbachev hostage and attempted to mount a coup.

The End of the Cold War: A Success for U.S. Policy

For forty-five years the United States blocked the Soviet path to world domination, holding the USSR in check while Communism gradually disintegrated from its own contradictions. President Reagan accelerated this process, and his successor skillfully managed the events surrounding the USSR's decline and fall. Soviet expert George Kennan wrote the script in 1947, noting that the inefficient and repressive Soviet system bore "the seeds of its own decay," and correctly predicting that "the United States has it in its power to increase enormously the strains under which Soviet policy must operate . . . and in this way to promote tendencies which must eventually find their outlet in either the breakup or the gradual mellowing of Soviet power."[7] Successive U.S. presidents followed Kennan's script. Ronald Reagan and George Bush presided over the happy ending in the final act. As historian John Lewis Gaddis says in praise of Reagan's role in ending the Cold War, "Strength . . . did lead to negotiations, bargaining chips did produce bargains, and 'hanging tough' did eventually pay off."[8]

---

1. Quoted in Bernard A. Weisberger, *Cold War, Cold Peace: The United States and Russia Since 1945*. Boston: Houghton Mifflin, 1984, p. 296.

2. John Spanier and Steven W. Hook, *American Foreign Policy Since World War II*, 14th ed. Washington, DC: CQ, 1998, p. 227.

3. Quoted in Thomas G. Paterson and Dennis Merrill, eds., *Major Problems in American Foreign Relations: Documents and Essays*, 4th ed. Lexington, MA: D.C. Heath, 1995, pp. 746, 753.

4. Quoted in Don Oberdorfer, *The Turn: From the Cold War to a New Era, the United States and the Soviet Union, 1983–1990*. New York: Poseidon, 1991, p. 395; Spanier and Hook, *American Foreign Policy Since World War II*, p. 251.

5. Michael R. Beschloss and Strobe Talbott, *At the Highest Levels: The Inside Story of the End of the Cold War*. Boston: Little, Brown, 1993, p. 135.

6. Quoted in Beschloss and Talbott, *At the Highest Levels*, p. 135.

7. Mr. X (George Kennan), "The Sources of Soviet Conduct," *Foreign Affairs*, Spring 1987, p. 868.

8. Quoted in Paterson and Merrill, *Major Problems in American Foreign Relations*, p. 738.

"The truth is that the West didn't win the Cold War at all. The Soviet Union lost it."

U.S. Policies in the 1980s Prolonged the Cold War

The Cold War ended because the Soviets selected a brave and innovative leader in 1985 who pursued bold reform at home and peace and reconciliation abroad. Soviet leader Mikhail Gorbachev took the initiative to break the cycle of mistrust and confrontation that had marked relations between the Soviet Union and the United States for four decades. The policies of Republican presidents Ronald Reagan and George Bush did not shape Gorbachev's conciliatory actions. In fact, the Republicans' confrontational policies threatened the USSR and frightened Soviet leaders, thus delaying the end of the Cold War. When the Cold War ended in 1991, it ended *despite* American actions, not because of them.

Western Influences on Soviet Behavior

The Soviet Union was influenced by broad international trends and certain Western ideas. But it was not Reagan's peace-through-strength approach, hard-line anti-Communism, or celebration of laissez-faire capitalism that influenced developments in the Soviet Union. Just the opposite. Soviet reformers were influenced by European Social Democrats (who, unlike

Reagan, favored expensive social welfare programs), peace
movements, and other liberal groups. Western culture also
played an important role in stimulating the changes in the
USSR that brought about the end of the Cold War. As political
scientists Daniel Deudney and G. John Ikenberry note, it was
not so much Western political ideas as the Western way of
life—affluence and popular culture—that "subverted the Soviet
vision." Deudney and Ikenberry are correct in claiming that
"Western popular culture—exemplified in rock and roll, television, film and blue jeans—seduced the communist world far
more effectively than ideological sermons by anti-communist
activists."[1] Still, the importance of outside influences was minor.
The critical sources of change were inside the Soviet Union.

Reformist Forces Within the Soviet Union

Conservatives give Reagan credit for bringing about changes
in Soviet policy, but it was mere coincidence that Reagan was
in office while historic changes occurred in the Soviet Union.
A middle class, which had been slowly but steadily growing in
the USSR, was quietly demanding economic reform and
greater openness in Soviet society. A new generation of Soviet
leaders was emerging, the first that had not come of age during the dreadful Stalin years. These leaders were much less
wedded to Communist orthodoxies than their predecessors.
Many had traveled extensively in the West and were less fearful of or hostile toward Westerners, greatly contrasting the
previous generation of Soviet leaders, many of whom had
never ventured outside the Communist world.

The thing that most prompted young leaders to consider
the path of reform was the terrible state of the Soviet economy. Economic growth had come to a standstill. Many foods,
consumer goods, and other products were in chronic short
supply, and citizens were forced to stand in line for hours to
get even the most basic goods. The Soviet Union lagged far
behind Western nations in advanced industries and technologies. As scholars John Spanier and Steven W. Hook assert,
economic life in the USSR had become a "textbook case" of

the ills of a state-controlled economy: "inefficiency, lack of productivity, unresponsiveness to consumer needs, and technological stagnation."[2]

Pressures for change came from both the bottom (the people) and the top (the leadership) of Soviet society. Gorbachev understood that old Communist ways were unsuited to life in the information age. State-controlled enterprises and farms were notoriously inefficient. The Communist-controlled bureaucracy that made key decisions about production was grossly unqualified to manage a modern economy. Gorbachev understood that the Soviet Union could not hope to be economically or technologically competitive in an interdependent world if information flows were drastically limited and access to computers and copying machines was severely restricted for political reasons.

Thus, Gorbachev embarked on a course of reform, promoting openness (called glasnost) in flows of information and restructuring (called perestroika) of the Soviet economy. To succeed he had to confront the massive apparatus of the Communist Party that was committed to the old ways out of self-interest (Communist elites benefited from numerous privileges) and as a matter of ideological faith. The weakening of the Communist old guard opened the way for far-reaching changes in both domestic and foreign policy.

Gorbachev's Policies Ended the Cold War

Gorbachev wanted to end the Cold War. He needed an end to tensions and global competition with the United States so that the Soviet Union could focus on domestic reform and divert resources from military spending to domestic restructuring. Gorbachev also sought to increase trade with the West, especially imports of high technology. These needs had nothing to do with American policies. They existed whether or not there was a Reagan Doctrine or an American Strategic Defense Initiative. Gorbachev would have worked to end the Cold War whether there was a hawk or a dove in the White House.

The Cold War ended because the Soviet Union made bold initiatives in all of the major policy areas that had caused tensions between Washington and Moscow. The changes that emerged from Gorbachev's new thinking in foreign and defense policy were truly extraordinary. Under Gorbachev defense spending was cut for the first time in decades. Nuclear arms control treaties were concluded on terms favorable to Western Europe and the United States. In Europe, where the Warsaw Pact fielded fifty thousand main battle tanks to the North Atlantic Treaty Organization's (NATO) twenty thousand, Gorbachev dealt away enormous superiority in conventional weapons in a treaty that would have been unthinkable to previous Soviet leaders, virtually eliminating any serious Soviet military threat to Western Europe in the process. Gorbachev effectively conceded Soviet defeat in Afghanistan and voluntarily withdrew from competition with the United States in the Third World. Gorbachev stood back and allowed Eastern European states to go their own way and even to abandon Communism in a series of democratic revolutions. And Gorbachev initiated human rights reforms that were unprecedented in the history of Communism.

These policy initiatives ended the Cold War by removing the sources of tension and competition between the United States and the Soviet Union. Gorbachev alone deserves the credit. Even William G. Hyland, a hawkish Soviet expert and former U.S. official, acknowledges that Gorbachev "was the crucial figure in ending the Cold War."[3]

Reagan's Policies Were Counterproductive

Not only does Reagan not deserve credit for ending the Cold War, he is also to blame for prolonging it. His bitterly anti-Soviet rhetoric and hard-line foreign and defense policies raised tensions and unnecessarily frightened Soviet leaders.

In his first three years in office, Reagan overreacted to Soviet actions in Afghanistan, Poland, and Central America. Reagan's rhetoric was shrill and hostile. The American president undiplomatically accused the Soviets of being willing to "lie, cheat, and steal" to get what they wanted, and he denounced Communism as the "focus of evil in the modern world" and the USSR as the "evil empire."[4]

Worst of all, Reagan's aggressive defense policies convinced Soviet leaders that the United States was preparing for war against the USSR. Reagan initiated the largest peacetime military buildup in American history, allowing the U.S. Defense Department to go on a "mindless spending spree,"[5] in the words of Soviet expert Raymond L. Garthoff. The Reagan administration spoke recklessly of the feasibility of limited nuclear war in Europe while bullying America's NATO partners into allowing the deployment of American intermediate-range missiles that the Soviets (and much of Western Europe) believed were designed to

Some critics feel that President Reagan's anti-Communist policies allowed the Cold War to continue.

fight rather than deter a nuclear war in Europe. U.S. nuclear modernization programs and especially Reagan's immensely costly Strategic Defense Initiative—which the Soviets saw as a potentially lethal neutralizer of their nuclear deterrent force—brought the United States "closer and closer to a military posture which seems to be designed solely and purposefully for first strike,"[6] as defense analyst Robert M. Bowman wrote at the time.

Because of U.S. policies under Reagan, the "Soviet perception of the likelihood of war increased sharply in 1981–84," according to Michael McGwire, a close student of Soviet military affairs. As McGwire says of the conciliatory style that developed in Soviet policy in 1987, "The crusading and confrontational policies of the first Reagan administration made it impossible for that favorable trend to emerge earlier and could easily have prevented it from emerging at all."[7]

Reagan's stubborn insistence on clinging to his Strategic Defense Initiative was an especially large obstacle to improved relations. At the Reykjavik, Iceland, summit conference in 1986, Reagan and Gorbachev were both prepared to conclude a treaty requiring the complete abolition of nuclear weapons, but what would have been a wondrous achievement failed because Reagan was unwilling to give up his initiative.

The Truth About the End of the Cold War

As international relations scholar John Mueller notes, all of the "calamities" that brought the Soviet Union down were "self-inflicted." Thus, Mueller concludes, "the truth is that the West didn't win the Cold War at all. The Soviet Union lost it."[8] Even Reaganites concede that the Soviet Union fell apart (in 1991) because of the fundamental and fatal flaws of its Communist system. But the Soviet Union's loss should not obscure a larger truth. Even before the breakup of the Soviet Union, Gorbachev was the courageous statesman who ended the Cold War.

1. Daniel Deudney and G. John Ikenberry, "Who Won the Cold War?" *Foreign Policy*, Summer 1992, p. 134.

2. John Spanier and Steven W. Hook, *American Foreign Policy Since World War II*, 14th ed. Washington, DC: CQ, 1998, p. 263.

3. William G. Hyland, *The Cold War: Fifty Years of Conflict*. New York: Random House, 1991, p. 201.

4. Quoted in Spanier and Hook, *American Foreign Policy Since World War II*, p. 213.

5. Raymond L. Garthoff, *Détente and Confrontation: American-Soviet Relations from Nixon to Reagan*. Washington, DC: Brookings, 1985, p. 1,064.

6. Quoted in John B. Harris and Eric Markusen, eds., *Nuclear Weapons and the Threat of Nuclear War*. New York: Harcourt Brace Jovanovich, 1986, p. 472.

7. Michael McGwire, *Perestroika and Soviet National Security*. Washington, DC: Brookings, 1991, pp. 381, 386.

8. John Mueller, "Enough Rope," *New Republic*, July 3, 1989, p. 14.

STUDY QUESTIONS

Author's note: Cold War historians spend their entire careers addressing questions such as these. Even the smallest points of debate are the subject of numerous studies that examine mountains of evidence. Use the viewpoints in this book to answer the questions posed here, but also consider the types of information that would add weight to your answers, such as more specific military data, speeches from political leaders, or more reliable, firsthand accounts of specific events.

Chapter 1

1. From the start, the Cold War was characterized by suspicion and distrust between the United States and the Soviet Union. Provide examples from the text of early incidents that spurred animosity between the superpowers.

2. Does it seem that American and Soviet leaders understood each other's aims and motives and that the Cold War was caused by real conflicting interests, or is it likely that misperceptions on one or both sides produced Cold War fears and suspicions? Provide evidence from the viewpoints to support your answer.

3. American leaders were convinced that there was a relationship between the Soviet Union's domestic and foreign policies, that a regime that oppressed its own people was a threat to other countries. Do you feel that the fact that the Soviet Union was a totalitarian country meant that it was an international threat as well?

Chapter 2

1. Throughout the Cold War, nuclear peace was a product of mutual terror. Neither superpower could defend itself from nuclear attack, and was thus compelled to rely on the threat of devastating retaliation (mutually assured destruction) to deter a nuclear attack by its rival. Do you feel that the strategy of nuclear deterrence is moral? Explain your answer. According to Viewpoints 1 and 2, were there realistic alternatives?

2. The threat of nuclear war hung over the world for more than four decades during the Cold War, yet, except for the use of two nuclear weapons by the United States at the end of World War II, nuclear weapons have not been used. Do you feel that this is evidence that nuclear weapons helped keep the Cold War a relatively bloodless

conflict, as defenders of nuclear deterrence claim, or that it was merely luck, as critics of nuclear weapons often claim? Explain your answer.

3. Both American and Soviet leaders were deeply concerned about the numbers of weapons each side had, as well as the specifics of their size, accuracy, etc. Critics charged that such factors were unimportant in light of the immense destructive power of even a small number of nuclear weapons. What do you think?

4. Why did U.S. presidents from Eisenhower to Nixon feel that U.S. intervention in Vietnam was necessary? In your opinion, were their concerns about "falling dominos" justified? Cite evidence from Viewpoints 2 and 3 to support your answer.

5. The Vietnam conflict stimulated a broader debate about whether "containment" of Communism should be applied globally, or only to the most strategically vital regions and countries, such as Europe and Japan. Do you think a strategy of limited containment might have been more successful, or, given U.S. concerns about Soviet totalitarianism, might it have been morally wrong to abandon less strategically important nations to Communist influence?

6. Citing examples from the text, give three reasons why détente failed.

7. Viewpoint 5 blames the failure of détente on the United States, while Viewpoint 6 puts the blame squarely on the Soviet Union. Which argument is more persuasive, and why?

Chapter 3

1. Based on the viewpoints, which leader—Mikhail Gorbachev or Ronald Reagan—played a greater role in ending the Cold War? Defend your answer.

2. Besides the leadership of Gorbachev and Reagan, what larger social and economic forces contributed to the end of the Cold War, according to the viewpoints?

APPENDIX

Excerpts from Original Cold War Documents

Document 1: The Yalta Conference: Declaration on Liberated Europe

In 1945, with victory over Nazi Germany looming, President Franklin Roosevelt met Soviet leader Joseph Stalin and British prime minister Winston Churchill at Yalta in the Crimea to discuss postwar arrangements. In the Declaration on Liberated Europe, Stalin agreed to the other two leaders' demand for a democratic future for Poland. When instead Poland became Communist, anti-Soviet sentiment in the West grew considerably. Yalta became a symbol of Soviet duplicity.

The following declaration has been approved:

The Premier of the Union of Soviet Socialist Republics, the Prime Minister of the United Kingdom and the President of the United States of America have consulted with each other in the common interests of the peoples of their countries and those of liberated Europe. They jointly declare their mutual agreement to concert during the temporary period of instability in liberated Europe the policies of their three governments in assisting the peoples of the former Axis satellite states of Europe to solve by democratic means their pressing political and economic problems.

The establishment of order in Europe and the rebuilding of national economic life must be achieved by processes which will enable the liberated peoples to destroy the last vestiges of Nazism and Fascism and to create democratic institutions of their own choice. This is a principle of the Atlantic Charter—the right of all peoples to choose the form of government under which they will live—the restoration of sovereign rights and self-government to those peoples who have been forcibly deprived of them by the aggressor nations.

To foster the conditions in which the liberated peoples may exercise these rights, the three governments will jointly assist the people in any European liberated state or former Axis satellite state in Europe where in their judgment conditions require (a) to establish conditions of internal peace; (b) to carry out emergency measures for the relief of distressed peoples; (c) to form interim governmental authorities broadly representative of all democratic elements in the population and pledged to the earliest possible establishment through free elections of governments responsive to the will of the people; and (d) to facilitate where necessary the holding of such elections.

The three governments will consult the other United Nations and provisional authorities or other governments in Europe when matters of direct interest to them are under consideration.

When, in the opinion of the three governments, conditions in any European liberated state or any former Axis satellite state in Europe make such action necessary, they will immediately consult together on the measures necessary to discharge the joint responsibilities set forth in this declaration.

By this declaration we reaffirm our faith in the principles of the Atlantic Charter, our pledges in the Declaration by the United Nations, and our determination to build in cooperation with other peace-loving nations world order under law, dedicated to peace, security, freedom and general well-being of all mankind.

In issuing this declaration, the Three Powers express the hope that the Provisional Government of the French Republic may be associated with them in the procedure suggested.

Yalta Conference Protocol of Proceedings, 1945.

Document 2: Churchill's Iron Curtain Speech

In 1946 former British prime minister Winston Churchill gave a speech in President Harry Truman's home state of Missouri in which he emphasized the human tragedy taking place in Eastern Europe as the Soviets consolidated their hold. He introduced the famous metaphor of "iron curtain" to depict the growing division between Eastern and Western Europe. Churchill's speech signified the growing Western alarm over Soviet conduct and the steady drift toward the Cold War.

A shadow has fallen upon the scenes so lately light by the Allied victory. Nobody knows what Soviet Russia and its Communist international organization intends to do in the immediate future, or what are the limits, if any, to their expansive and proselytizing tendencies. I have a strong admiration and regard for the valiant Russian people and for my wartime comrade, Marshall Stalin. There is deep sympathy and goodwill in Britain—and I doubt not here also—towards the peoples of all the Russias and a resolve to persevere through many differences and rebuffs in establishing lasting friendships. We understand the Russian need to be secure on her western frontiers by the removal of all possibility of German aggression. We welcome Russia to her rightful place among the leading nations of the world. We welcome her flag upon the seas. Above all, we welcome, or should welcome, constant, frequent and growing contacts between the Russian people and our own people on both sides of the Atlantic. It is my duty however, for I am sure you would wish me to state the facts as I see them to you. It is my duty to place before you certain facts about the present position in Europe.

From Stettin in the Baltic to Trieste in the Adriatic an *iron curtain* has descended across the Continent. Behind that line lie all the capitals of the ancient states of Central and Eastern Europe. Warsaw, Berlin,

Prague, Vienna, Budapest, Belgrade, Bucharest and Sofia, all these famous cities and the populations around them lie in what I must call the Soviet sphere, and all are subject in one form or another, not only to Soviet influence but to a very high and, in some cases, increasing measure of control from Moscow. Athens alone—Greece with its immortal glories—is free to decide its future at an election under British, American and French observation. The Russian-dominated Polish Government has been encouraged to make enormous and wrongful inroads upon Germany, and mass expulsions of millions of Germans on a scale grievous and undreamed-of are now taking place. The Communist parties, which were very small in all these Eastern States of Europe, have been raised to pre-eminence and power far beyond their numbers and are seeking everywhere to obtain totalitarian control. Police governments are prevailing in nearly every case, and so far, except in Czechoslovakia, there is no true democracy.

Turkey and Persia are both profoundly alarmed and disturbed at the claims which are being made upon them and at the pressure being exerted by the Moscow Government. . . .

In a great number of countries, far from the Russian frontiers and throughout the world, Communist fifth columns are established and work in complete unity and absolute obedience to the directions they receive from the Communist center. . . .

On the other hand, ladies and gentlemen, I repulse the idea that a new war is inevitable; still more that it is imminent. It is because I am sure that our fortunes are still in our own hands and that we hold the power to save the future, that I feel the duty to speak out now that I have the occasion and the opportunity to do so. I do not believe that Soviet Russia desires war. What they desire is the fruits of war and the indefinite expansion of their power and doctrines. But what we have to consider here today while time remains, is the permanent prevention of war and the establishment of conditions of freedom and democracy as rapidly as possible in all countries. Our difficulties and dangers will not be removed by closing our eyes to them. They will not be removed by mere waiting to see what happens; nor will they be removed by a policy of appeasement. What is needed is a settlement, and the longer this is delayed, the more difficult it will be and the greater our dangers will become.

From what I have seen of our Russian friends and Allies during the war, I am convinced that there is nothing for which they have less respect than for weakness, especially military weakness. . . .

If the population of the English-speaking Commonwealths be added to that of the United States with all that such co-operation implies in the air, on the sea, all over the globe and in science and in industry, and in moral force, there will be no quivering, precarious balance of power to offer its temptation to ambition or adventure. On the contrary there will be an overwhelming assurance of security.

Winston Churchill, "Iron Curtain" speech, Fulton, Missouri, March 5, 1946.

Document 3: The Truman Doctrine

In his quest for congressional approval for aid for anticommunist forces in Greece and Turkey, in March 1947 President Harry Truman issued one of the most famous presidential declarations of the Cold War: "It must be the policy of the United States to support free peoples who are resisting attempted subjugation by armed minorities or by outside pressures." Truman's speech to Congress clearly revealed the deepening American fears of the Soviet Union, and it marked the beginning of the policy of containment.

The United States has received from the Greek Government an urgent appeal for financial and economic assistance. . . . The very existence of the Greek state is today threatened by the terrorist activities of several thousand armed men, led by communists, who defy the Government's authority at a number of points, particularly along the northern boundaries. . . . Greece must have assistance if it is to become a self-supporting and self-respecting democracy. . . . There is no other country to which democratic Greece can turn. . . . Greece's neighbor, Turkey, also deserves our attention.

The future of Turkey as an independent and economically sound state is clearly no less important to the freedom-loving peoples of the world than the future of Greece. . . .

As in the case of Greece, if Turkey is to have the assistance it needs, the United States must supply it. We are the only country able to provide that help. . . . Totalitarian regimes imposed on free peoples, by direct or indirect aggression, undermine the foundations of international peace and hence the security of the United States. . . .

At the present moment in the world history nearly every nation must choose between alternative ways of life. The choice is too often not a free one.

One way of life is based upon the will of the majority and is distinguished by free institutions, representing government, free elections, guarantees of individual liberty, freedom of speech and religion, and freedom from political oppression.

The second way of life is based upon the will of the minority forcibly imposed upon the majority. It relies on terror and oppression, a controlled press and radio, fixed elections, and the suppression of personal freedoms.

I believe that it must be the policy of the United States to support free peoples who are resisting attempted subjugation by armed minorities or by outside pressures.

I believe that we must assist peoples to work out their own destinies in their own way.

I believe that our help should be primarily through economic and financial aid which is essential to economic stability and orderly political processes. . . .

It is necessary only to glance at a map to realize that the survival and integrity of the Greek nation are of grave importance in a much wider situation. If Greece should fall under the control of an armed minority, the effect upon its neighbor Turkey, would be immediate and serious. Confusion and disorder might well spread throughout the entire Middle East. . . .

Should we fail to aid Greece and Turkey in this fateful hour, the effect will be far reaching to the West as well as to the East.

Harry S. Truman, special message to the Congress on Greece and Turkey, March 12, 1947.

Document 4: NSC-68

NSC-68 was a lengthy top secret report to President Harry Truman, issued by the National Security Council (NSC) in April 1950. It paints a stark picture of Soviet leaders bent on world domination, emphasizing the military advantages possessed by the USSR. NSC-68 made a number of policy recommendations for the United States, the most important of which called for substantial increases in military spending. Two months after the report's release, Communist North Korea invaded non-Communist South Korea, leading President Harry Truman to endorse the findings and recommendations of NSC-68. American defense spending nearly quadrupled and U.S.-Soviet relations spiraled downward. The text remained classified until 1975.

The Soviet Union, unlike previous aspirants to hegemony, is animated by a new fanatic faith, anti-thetical to our own, and seeks to impose its absolute authority over the rest of the world. Conflict has, therefore, become endemic and is waged, on the part of the Soviet Union, by violent or non-violent methods in accordance with the dictates of expediency. With the development of increasingly terrifying weapons of mass destruction, every individual faces the ever-present possibility of annihilation should the conflict enter the phase of total war. . . .

Fundamental Design of the Kremlin

The fundamental design of those who control the Soviet Union and the international communist movement is to retain and solidify their absolute power, first in the Soviet Union and second in the areas now under their control. In the minds of the Soviet leaders, however, achievement of this design requires the dynamic extension of their authority and the ultimate elimination of any effective opposition to their authority. . . .

The United States, as the principal center of power in the non-Soviet world and the bulwark of opposition to Soviet expansion, is the principal enemy whose integrity and vitality must be subverted or destroyed by one means or another if the Kremlin is to achieve its fundamental design.

The Kremlin regards the United States as the only major threat to the conflict between the idea of freedom under a government of laws and the idea of slavery under the grim oligarchy of the Kremlin. . . .

The Soviet Union is developing the military capacity to support its design for world domination. The Soviet Union actually possesses armed forces far in excess of those necessary to defend its national territory. These armed forces are probably not yet considered by the Soviet Union to be sufficient to initiate a war which would involve the United States. This excessive strength, coupled now with an atomic capability, provides the Soviet Union with great coercive power for use in time of peace in furtherance of its objectives and serves as a deterrent to the victims of its aggression from taking any action in opposition to its tactics which would risk war. . . .

U.S. Soviet Policy
As for the policy of "containment," it is one which seeks by all means short of war to (1) block further expansion of Soviet power, (2) expose the falsities of Soviet pretensions, (3) induce a retraction of the Kremlin's control and influence, and (4) in general, so foster the seeds of destruction within the Soviet system that the Kremlin is brought at least to the point of modifying its behavior to conform to generally accepted international standards. . . .

At the same time, it is essential to the successful conduct of a policy of "containment" that we always leave open the possibility of negotiation with the USSR.

A more rapid build-up of political, economic, and military strength and thereby of confidence in the free world than is now contemplated is the only course which is consistent with progress toward achieving our fundamental purpose. The frustration of the Kremlin design requires the free world to develop a successfully functioning political and economic system and a vigorous political offensive against the Soviet Union. These, in turn, require an adequate military shield under which they can develop . . . a firm policy intended to check and to roll back the Kremlin's drive for world domination. . . .

A comprehensive and decisive program to win the peace and frustrate the Kremlin design should be so designed that it can be sustained for as long as necessary to achieve our national objectives. It would probably involve:

1. The development of an adequate political and economic framework for the achievement of our long-range objectives.

2. A substantial increase in expenditures for military purposes. . . .

3. A substantial increase in military assistance programs. . . .

4. Some increase in economic assistance programs. . . .

5. A concerted attack on the problem of the United States balance of payments. . . .

6. Development of programs designed to build and maintain confidence among other peoples in our strength and resolution, and to wage overt psychological warfare calculated to encourage mass defections from Soviet allegiance and to frustrate the Kremlin design in other ways.

7. Intensification of affirmative and timely measures and operations by covert means in the fields of economic warfare and political and psychological warfare with a view to fomenting and supporting unrest and revolt in selected strategic satellite countries.

8. Development of internal security and civilian defense programs.

9. Improvement and intensification of intelligence activities.

10. Reduction of Federal expenditures for purposes other than defense and foreign assistance, if necessary by the deferment of certain desirable programs.

11. Increased taxes. . . .

Time is short, however, and the risks of war attendant upon a decision to build up strength will steadily increase the longer we defer it. . . .

In particular, the United States now faces the contingency that within the next four or five years the Soviet Union will possess the military capability of delivering a surprise atomic attack of such weight that the United States must have substantially increased general air, ground, and sea strength, atomic capabilities, and air and civilian defenses to deter war and to provide reasonable assurance, in the event of war, that it could survive the initial blow and go on to the eventual attainment of its objectives.

The whole success of the proposed program hangs ultimately on recognition by this Government, the American people, and all free peoples, that the cold war is in fact a real war in which the survival of the free world is at stake.

National Security Council no. 68: United States Objectives and Programs for National Security, April 14, 1950.

Document 5: Secretary of State John Foster Dulles Explains Massive Retaliation

In 1954 Secretary of State John Foster Dulles made a controversial speech in which he proposed a greater reliance on nuclear weapons to counter threats from China and the Soviet Union. The recently ended Korean War had triggered an enormous increase in U.S. defense spending, which President Dwight Eisenhower believed was economically unsustainable. Secretary of State John Foster Dulles outlined a lower-cost deterrent strategy based on America's "massive retaliatory power," clearly referring to nuclear weapons. The press soon dubbed the controversial strategy "massive retaliation."

The Soviet Communists are planning for what they call "an entire historical era," and we should do the same. They seek, through many types of maneuvers, gradually to divide and weaken the free nations by overextending them in efforts which, as Lenin put it, are "beyond their strength, so that they come to practical bankruptcy." Then, said Lenin, "our victory is assured." Then, said Stalin, will be "the moment for the decisive blow."

In the face of this strategy, measures cannot be judged adequate merely because they ward off an immediate danger. It is essential to do this, but it is also essential to do so without exhausting ourselves.

When the Eisenhower administration applied this test, we felt that some transformations were needed.

It is not sound military strategy permanently to commit U.S. land forces to Asia to a degree that leaves us no strategic reserves.

It is not sound economics, or good foreign policy, to support permanently other countries; for in the long run, that creates as much ill will as good will.

Also, it is not sound to become permanently committed to military expenditures so vast that they lead to "practical bankruptcy." . . .

We need allies and collective security. Our purpose is to make these relations more effective, less costly. This can be done by placing more reliance on deterrent power and less dependence on local defensive power.

This is accepted practice so far as local communities are concerned. We keep locks on our doors, but we do not have an armed guard in every home. We rely principally on a community security system so well equipped to punish any who break in and steal that, in fact, would-be aggressors are generally deterred. That is the modern way of getting maximum protection at a bearable cost.

What the Eisenhower administration seeks is a similar international security system. We want, for ourselves and the other free nations, a maximum deterrent at a bearable cost.

Local defense will always be important. But there is no local defense which alone will contain the mighty landpower of the Communist world. Local defenses must be reinforced by the further deterrent of massive retaliatory power. A potential aggressor must know that he cannot always prescribe battle conditions that suit him. Otherwise, for example, a potential aggressor, who is glutted with manpower, might be tempted to attack in confidence that resistance would be confined to manpower. He might be tempted to attack in places where his superiority was decisive.

The way to deter aggression is for the free community to be willing and able to respond vigorously at places and with means of its own choosing.

So long as our basic policy concepts were unclear, our military leaders could not be selective in building our military power. If an enemy could pick his time and place and method of warfare—and if our policy was to remain the traditional one of meeting aggression by direct and local opposition—then we needed to be ready to fight in the Arctic and in the Tropics; in Asia, the Near East, and Europe; by sea, by land, and by air; with old weapons and with new weapons. . . .

But before military planning could be changed, the President and his advisers, as represented by the National Security Council, had to take some basic policy decisions. This has been done. The basic decision was to depend primarily upon a great capacity to retaliate, instantly, by means and at places of our choosing.

John Foster Dulles, "Massive Retaliation" speech, January 12, 1954.

Document 6: Kennedy's Address to the Nation During the Cuban Missile Crisis

In one of the most tense periods in the nation's history, President Kennedy gave a televised address explaining the actions he was taking to deal with the 1962 Soviet deployment of nuclear missiles in Cuba. Kennedy demanded the removal of the missiles and announced the imposition of a naval blockade of Cuba, raising the possibility of a violent clash at sea between the superpowers or a Soviet countermove against Berlin. Under the shadow of possible nuclear war, the world watched and waited for several days. In the end Moscow announced it would remove the missiles, ending the crisis.

Good evening, my fellow citizens:

This Government, as promised, has maintained the closest surveillance of the Soviet military buildup on the island of Cuba. Within the past week, unmistakable evidence has established the fact that a series of offensive missile sites is now in preparation on that imprisoned island. The purpose of these bases can be none other than to provide a nuclear strike capability against the Western Hemisphere. . . .

Soviet Provocation

This secret, swift, and extraordinary buildup of Communist missiles—in an area well known to have a special and historical relationship to the United States and the nations of the Western Hemisphere, in violation of Soviet assurances, and in defiance of American and hemispheric policy—this sudden, clandestine decision to station strategic weapons for the first time outside of Soviet soil—is a deliberately provocative and unjustified change in the status quo which cannot be accepted by this country, if our courage and our commitments are ever to be trusted again by either friend or foe.

The 1930's taught us a clear lesson: aggressive conduct, if allowed to go unchecked and unchallenged, ultimately leads to war. This nation is opposed to war. We are also true to our word. Our unswerving objective, therefore, must be to prevent the use of these missiles against this or any other country, and to secure their withdrawal or elimination from the Western Hemisphere.

Our policy has been one of patience and restraint, as befits a peaceful and powerful nation, which leads a worldwide alliance. We have been determined not to be diverted from our central concerns by mere irritants and fanatics. But now further action is required—and it is under way; and these actions may only be the beginning. We will not prematurely or unnecessarily risk the costs of worldwide nuclear war in which even the fruits of victory would be ashes in our mouth—but neither will we shrink from that risk at any time it must be faced. . . .

The U.S. Response

To halt this offensive buildup, a strict quarantine on all offensive military equipment under shipment to Cuba is being initiated. . . . I call upon Chairman [Nikita] Khrushchev to halt and eliminate this clandestine, reckless, and provocative threat to world peace and to stable relations between our two nations. I call upon him further to abandon this course of world domination, and to join in an historic effort to end the perilous arms race and to transform the history of man. He has an opportunity now to move the world back from the abyss of destruction. . . .

Any hostile move anywhere in the world against the safety and freedom of peoples to whom we are committed—including in particular the brave people of West Berlin—will be met by whatever action is needed. . . .

My fellow citizens: let no one doubt that this is a difficult and dangerous effort on which we have set out. No one can foresee precisely what course it will take or what costs or casualties will be incurred. Many months of sacrifice and self-discipline lie ahead—months in which both our patience and our will will be tested—months in which many threats and denunciations will keep us aware of our dangers. But the greatest danger of all would be to do nothing.

John F. Kennedy, radio and television address on the Cuban missile crisis, October 22, 1962.

Document 7: The Brezhnev Doctrine

In August 1968 East-West relations were roiled by a Soviet-led Warsaw Pact intervention in Czechoslovakia, a member state of the Pact. Soviet tanks were sent to remove reformist leaders in Prague. The following month, the article excerpted below appeared in the Russian newspaper Pravda *justifying the intervention, citing threats to Communism in Czechoslovakia and claiming that the needs of the socialist community took precedence over Czechoslovakia's right to sovereignty and independence. This claim, expressed on several occasions by Soviet leader Leonid Brezhnev, was dubbed the Brezhnev Doctrine. For the West, the doctrine epitomized the worst features of Soviet domination of Eastern Europe, and for twenty years was a stumbling block in U.S.-Soviet relations until Mikhail Gorbachev abruptly reversed course in 1989.*

There is no doubt that the peoples of the socialist countries and the Communist parties have and must have freedom to determine their country's path of development. However, any decision of theirs must damage neither socialism in their own country, nor the fundamental interests of the other socialist countries, nor the world-wide workers' movement, which is waging a struggle for socialism. This means that every Communist party is responsible not only to its own people but also to all the socialist countries and to the entire Communist movement. Whoever forgets this is placing sole emphasis on the autonomy and independence of Communist parties, lapsing into one-sidedness, and shirking his internationalist obligations. . . .

Each Communist party is free to apply the principles of Marxism-Leninism and socialism in its own country, but it cannot deviate from these principles (if, of course, it remains a Communist party). In concrete terms this means primarily that no Communist party can fail to take into account in its activities such a decisive fact of our time as the struggle between the two antithetical social systems—capitalism and socialism. This struggle is an objective fact that does not depend on the will of people and is conditioned by the division of the world into the two antithetical social systems. . . .

The weakening of any link in the world socialist system has a direct effect on all the socialist countries, which cannot be indifferent. Thus, the anti-socialist forces in Czechoslovakia were in essence using talk about the right to self-determination to cover up demands for so-called neutrality and the CSSR's [Czechoslovak Soviet Socialist Republic] withdrawal from the socialist commonwealth. But implementation of such "self-determination," i.e., Czechoslovakia's separation from the socialist commonwealth, would run counter to Czechoslovakia's fundamental interests and would harm the other socialist countries. Such "self-determination," as a result of which NATO troops might approach Soviet borders and the commonwealth of European socialist countries could be dismembered, in fact infringes on the vital interest of these countries' peoples, and fundamentally contradicts the right of these peoples to socialist self-determination. The Soviet Union and other socialist states, in fulfilling their internationalist duty to the fraternal peoples of Czechoslovakia and defending their own socialist gains, had to act and did act in resolute opposition to the antisocialist forces in Czechoslovakia.

Sergei Kovalev, *Pravda*, September 26, 1968.

Document 8: The 1972 U.S.-Soviet Agreement on Basic Principles

U.S.-Soviet Agreement on Basic Principles was one of the agreements signed at the Moscow summit at the height of détente. The agreement became a yardstick by which the United States judged Soviet conduct. In Washington's view, the agreement's requirement that both sides exercise restraint while avoiding the pursuit of unilateral advantage and military confrontations committed the Soviets to curbing their expansionist activities in the Third World. The Nixon administration also believed that the agreement's wording nullified the Brezhnev Doctrine. Moscow subsequently took many actions that the United States considered inconsistent with the Basic Principles Agreement, leading to a hardening of anti-Soviet sentiment in the United States.

The United States of America and the Union of Soviet Socialist Republics, . . . Have agreed as follows:

First. They will proceed from the common determination that in the nuclear age there is no alternative to conducting their mutual relations on the basis of peaceful coexistence. Differences in ideology and in the social systems of the USA and the USSR are not obstacles to the bilateral development of normal relations based on the principles of sovereignty, equality, non-interference in internal affairs and mutual advantage.

Second. The USA and the USSR attach major importance to preventing the development of situations capable of causing a dangerous exacerbation of their relations. Therefore, they will do their utmost to avoid military confrontations and to prevent the outbreak of nuclear war. They will always exercise restraint in their mutual relations, and will be prepared to negotiate and settle differences by peaceful means. Discussions and negotiations on outstanding issues will be conducted in a spirit of reciprocity, mutual accommodation and mutual benefit.

Both sides recognize that efforts to obtain unilateral advantage at the expense of the other, directly or indirectly, are inconsistent with these objectives. The prerequisites for maintaining and strengthening peaceful rela-

tions between the USA and USSR are the recognition of the security interests of the Parties based on the principle of equality and the renunciation of
the use or threat of force.

Third. The USA and the USSR have a special responsibility, as do other
countries which are permanent members of the United Nations Security
Council, to do everything in their power so that conflicts or situations will
not arise which would serve to increase international tensions. Accordingly,
they will seek to promote conditions in which all countries will live in peace
and security and will not be subject to outside interference in their internal
affairs. . . .

Eleventh. The USA and the USSR make no claim for themselves and
would not recognize the claims of anyone else to any special rights or advantages in world affairs. They recognize the sovereign equality of all states.

Basic Principals of Relations Between the United States of America and the Union of Soviet Socialist
Republics, May 29, 1972.

Document 9: The Carter Doctrine

*President Jimmy Carter devoted much of his January 1980 State of the Union
address to the Soviet Union's large-scale military intervention in Afghanistan a
month earlier. The Soviet intervention represented the first large-scale Soviet operation outside the Warsaw Pact area since World War II, and it brought Soviet
power closer to the oil-rich Persian Gulf. In the key line in the speech and what came
to be called the Carter Doctrine, the president committed the United States to defend
the Persian Gulf by "any means necessary, including military force."*

The Soviet Union has taken a radical and an aggressive new step. It's using
its great military power against a relatively defenseless nation. The implications of the Soviet invasion of Afghanistan could pose the most serious
threat to the peace since the Second World War. . . .

While this invasion continues, we and the other nations of the world cannot conduct business as usual with the Soviet Union. That's why the United
States has imposed stiff economic penalties on the Soviet Union. . . .

The Soviet Union is going to have to answer some basic questions: Will
it help promote a more stable international environment in which its own
legitimate, peaceful concerns can be pursued? Or will it continue to expand
its military power far beyond its genuine security needs, and use that power
for colonial conquest? The Soviet Union must realize that its decision to use
military force in Afghanistan will be costly to every political and economic
relationship it values.

The region which is now threatened by Soviet troops in Afghanistan is
of great strategic importance: It contains more than two-thirds of the
world's exportable oil. The Soviet effort to dominate Afghanistan has
brought Soviet military forces to within 300 miles of the Indian Ocean and
close to the Straits of Hormuz, a waterway through which most of the

world's oil must flow. The Soviet Union is now attempting to consolidate a strategic position, therefore, that poses a grave threat to the free movement of Middle East oil.

This situation demands careful thought, steady nerves, and resolute action, not only for this year but for many years to come. It demands collective efforts to meet this new threat to security in the Persian Gulf and in Southwest Asia. It demands the participation of all those who rely on oil from the Middle East and who are concerned with global peace and stability. And it demands consultation and close cooperation with countries in the area which might be threatened.

Meeting this challenge will take national will, diplomatic and political wisdom, economic sacrifice, and, of course, military capability. We must call on the best that is in us to preserve the security of this crucial region.

Let our position be absolutely clear: An attempt by any outside force to gain control of the Persian Gulf region will be regarded as an assault on the vital interests of the United States of America, and such an assault will be repelled by any means necessary, including military force.

Jimmy Carter, State of the Union address, January 23, 1980.

Document 10: Reagan's Evil Empire Speech

President Ronald Reagan revealed his strongly anti-Soviet views in this 1983 speech before a gathering of evangelical Christians. Critics claimed that Reagan contributed to worsening U.S.-Soviet relations by calling the Soviets an "evil empire," while supporters praised the president for his no-holds-barred straight talk.

During my first press conference as president, in answer to a direct question, I pointed out that, as good Marxist-Leninists, the Soviet leaders have openly and publicly declared that the only morality they recognize is that which will further their cause, which is world revolution. I think I should point out I was only quoting Lenin, their guiding spirit, who said in 1920 that they repudiate all morality that proceeds from supernatural ideas—that's their name for religion—or ideas that are outside class conceptions. Morality is entirely subordinate to the interests of class war. And everything is moral that is necessary for the annihilation of the old, exploiting social order and for uniting the proletariat.

Well, I think the refusal of many influential people to accept this elementary fact of Soviet doctrine illustrates a historical reluctance to see totalitarian powers for what they are. We saw this phenomenon in the 1930s. We see it too often today.

This doesn't mean we should isolate ourselves and refuse to seek an understanding with them. I intend to do everything I can to persuade them of our peaceful intent, to remind them that it was the West that refused to use its nuclear monopoly in the forties and fifties for territorial gain and which now proposes a 50-percent cut in strategic ballistic missiles and the elimination of an entire class of land-based, intermediate-range nuclear missiles.

At the same time, however, they must be made to understand we will never compromise our principles and standards. We will never give away our freedom. We will never abandon our belief in God. And we will never stop searching for a genuine peace. But we can assure none of these things America stands for through the so-called nuclear freeze solutions proposed by some.

The truth is that a freeze now would be a very dangerous fraud, for that is merely the illusion of peace. The reality is that we must find peace through strength.

I would agree to a freeze if only we could freeze the Soviets' global desires. A freeze at current levels of weapons would remove any incentive for the Soviets to negotiate seriously in Geneva and virtually end our chances to achieve the major arms reductions which we have proposed. Instead, they would achieve their objectives through the freeze.

A freeze would reward the Soviet Union for its enormous and unparalleled military buildup. It would prevent the essential and long overdue modernization of United States and allied defenses and would leave our aging forces increasingly vulnerable. And an honest freeze would require extensive prior negotiations on the systems and numbers to be limited and on the measures to ensure effective verification and compliance. And the kind of a freeze that has been suggested would be virtually impossible to verify. Such a major effort would divert us completely from our current negotiations on achieving substantial reductions. . . .

Let us pray for the salvation of all of those who live in that totalitarian darkness—pray they will discover the joy of knowing God. But until they do, let us be aware that while they preach the supremacy of the state, declare its omnipotence over individual man, and predict its eventual domination of all peoples on the earth, they are the focus of evil in the modern world. . . .

So, in your discussions of the nuclear freeze proposals, I urge you to beware the temptation of pride—the temptation of blithely declaring yourselves above it all and label both sides equally at fault, to ignore the facts of history and the aggressive impulses of an evil empire, to simply call the arms race a giant misunderstanding and thereby remove yourself from the struggle between right and wrong and good and evil.

Ronald Reagan, remarks at the Annual Convention of the National Association of Evangelicals, March 8, 1983.

CHRONOLOGY

1914
World War I starts.

1917
The Russian Revolution, led by Vladimir Lenin's Bolshevik Party, creates the world's first Communist regime; Communist Russia quits the war effort against imperial Germany.

1918
Civil war erupts in Russia; Japan, Britain, France, and the United States intervene militarily against the Bolsheviks.

1923
Lenin dies; Joseph Stalin takes over.

1928–1929
Stalin orders the forced collectivization of farms in the Ukraine and famine ensues.

1933
Hitler comes to power in Germany; Franklin D. Roosevelt recognizes the Soviet Union and establishes diplomatic relations; the United States is the last Western power to do so.

1937–1938
Millions die in the USSR as Stalin "purges" the nation of suspected anti-Communists.

1939
In August the Soviet Union and Nazi Germany sign the Molotov–von Ribbentropp Nonaggression Pact; the treaty enables the USSR to occupy eastern Poland; Britain and France declare war on Germany.

1940
The Soviet Union annexes the Baltic countries of Estonia, Latvia, and Lithuania.

1941
The Soviet Union signs a nonaggression treaty with Japan; Hitler launches Operation Barbarossa, a massive invasion of the Soviet Union, making the Soviets informal allies of the Western powers;

on December 7 Japan attacks Pearl Harbor, and the United States enters the war; the Soviet Union, Britain, and the United States become formal allies.

1942
Roosevelt promises Stalin the earliest possible opening of a second front against Germany.

1943
Roosevelt, Winston Churchill, and Stalin meet for the first time to begin planning for the postwar world.

1945
Roosevelt, Churchill, and Stalin meet at Yalta, agreeing to changes in borders and free democratic elections in Europe; Roosevelt dies and Harry Truman becomes president; Germany surrenders; Soviet Red Army troops occupy Poland, Hungary, Czechoslovakia, Romania, Bulgaria, and eastern Germany; Truman, Churchill, and Stalin meet at Potsdam for further discussions over the future of Poland and Germany; the United States successfully tests the world's first atomic bomb and subsequently drops atomic bombs on the Japanese cities of Hiroshima and Nagasaki; Japan surrenders, ending World War II.

1946
Stalin delivers a harsh speech predicting war and places the Soviet economy on a long-term war-footing; former British prime minister Winston Churchill delivers a speech in Fulton, Missouri, warning that an "iron curtain" is falling across Europe; U.S.-Soviet negotiations over the World War II peace settlement stall.

1947
The United States offers aid to the British anti-Communist forces in the Greek civil war; the result is the Truman Doctrine, a statement of U.S. support for anti-Communism everywhere; writing as "Mr. X" in the prestigious journal *Foreign Affairs*, George Kennan calls for containment of Soviet expansionism; containment becomes the pillar of U.S. foreign policy for four decades; Secretary of State George Marshall announces the Marshall Plan for massive U.S. economic aid to Europe.

1948

Communists take over Czechoslovakia; the Soviets impose a blockade on road and rail routes to West Berlin; the United States responds by airlifting food and supplies into Berlin.

1949

The North Atlantic Treaty Organization (NATO) is formed; members include the United States, Canada, Britain, France, Italy, the Netherlands, Belgium, Luxembourg, Denmark, Norway, Portugal, and Iceland; the Soviet Union ends the Berlin blockade; West Germany regains its independence under a democratic constitution; the Soviet Union tests its first atomic bomb; revolution in China brings Communists to power under Mao Tse-tung.

1950

The Soviet Union and China sign a treaty of alliance; Senator Joseph McCarthy begins his campaign of accusations that there are Communist sympathizers in the U.S. government; the top-secret document NSC-68 warns of a Soviet menace and calls for vigorous response, including a large increase in defense expenditures; Communist-backed North Korea invades South Korea; under the banner of the United Nations, the United States comes to the defense of South Korea.

1952

Britain becomes a nuclear power; Dwight Eisenhower is elected president.

1953

Stalin dies; Nikita Khrushchev soon emerges as the paramount Soviet leader; an armistice is signed in the Korean War; the Soviet Union tests the hydrogen bomb.

1954

The United States tests the hydrogen bomb; France is defeated at Dien Bien Phu and is driven out of Indochina; the Geneva Conference divides Vietnam at seventeenth parallel; the Southeast Asian Treaty Organization is formed; members include the United States, Britain, France, Australia, New Zealand, Thailand, Pakistan, and the Philippines; the United States signs treaty of alliance with South Korea and Taiwan; Germany joins NATO; the Warsaw Pact is created; members include the Soviet Union, East Germany, Poland, Hungary, Czechoslovakia, Romania, Bulgaria, and Albania (until 1961).

1955

Eisenhower and Khrushchev meet for the first time in Geneva, Switzerland.

1956

Khrushchev denounces Stalin's "crimes" in a secret speech at the Communist Party's twentieth party congress; there is crisis over the Suez Canal as France, Britain, and Israel attack Egypt; Washington opposes the attack; Soviet forces crush a rebellion in Hungary.

1957

The Soviet Union tests the intercontinental-range ballistic missile and puts two Sputnik satellites in space, alarming the United States; the Eisenhower Doctrine commits the United States to protect Middle Eastern countries from Soviet aggression.

1958

Tensions begin to rise between China and the Soviet Union; Khrushchev demands that the United States withdraw its troops from Berlin.

1959

Communist revolutionary leader Fidel Castro seizes power in Cuba; Khrushchev visits the United States.

1960

Soviets announce they have shot down an American U-2 spy plane; Eisenhower denies it was a spy plane; the Paris summit conference collapses; John F. Kennedy is elected president.

1961

Kennedy proposes the Alliance for Progress, a large-scale aid program for Latin America; Kennedy and Khrushchev meet for the first time in Vienna, Austria; Khrushchev calls for support for wars of "national liberation," and demands Western withdrawal from Berlin; the Berlin Wall is erected after a U.S.-Soviet face-off of tanks at Checkpoint Charlie.

1962

In October the Cuban missile crisis unfolds and is defused.

1963

Kennedy calls for a relaxation of tensions with the Soviets; the United States and the Soviet Union sign the "hot line" agreement and the

Nuclear Test Ban Treaty; U.S. involvement in Vietnam escalates; Kennedy is assassinated, and Lyndon Johnson becomes president.

1964
Congress passes the Gulf of Tonkin Resolution authorizing the president to take military action in Vietnam; China becomes a nuclear power; Khrushchev is ousted; Leonid Brezhnev soon emerges as the Soviet leader.

1965
The United States bombs North Vietnam and sends the first combat forces to South Vietnam; the U.S. Marines conduct an anti-Communist intervention in the Dominican Republic.

1967
The Arab-Israeli Six-Day War erupts; President Johnson meets with Soviet premier Aleksey Kosygin in Glassboro, New Jersey.

1968
North Vietnam's massive Tet offensive leads to military success but political defeat for the United States, leading to increased demands for U.S. withdrawal; Soviet troops crush Czechoslovakia's "Prague Spring" movement; Paris peace talks on Vietnam begin; Richard Nixon is elected president after Johnson decides not to seek reelection because of Vietnam.

1969
Nixon begins U.S. troop reductions from Vietnam; the Sino-Soviet split intensifies after clashes between China and the USSR along the Ussuri River; the Soviets proclaim the Brezhnev Doctrine, asserting that the needs of the international socialist community have precedence over sovereignty of member states—it effectively announces the complete Soviet dominance over satellite nations in Eastern Europe; Strategic Arms Limitation Talks (SALT) begin.

1970
President Nixon unfurls the Nixon Doctrine, proclaiming that U.S. allies must play a greater role in their own defense.

1972
Nixon visits China; détente reaches its zenith as Nixon and Brezhnev sign the Anti-Ballistic Missile treaty, SALT I, the Basic Principles Agreement, and a U.S.-Soviet trade pact at a summit in

Moscow; Nixon is reelected; the Paris peace talks over Vietnam break down; Nixon orders heavy bombing of North Vietnam.

1973
The Vietnam peace agreement is concluded; the Cold War shifts to South America as the United States helps engineer a coup against Chile's socialist president Salvador Allende; the Yom Kippur War erupts in the Middle East; Congress passes the War Powers Act over Nixon's veto, constraining the president's ability to use force.

1974
A military coup in Ethiopia brings a Marxist regime to power; Portuguese colonial rule over the African countries of Angola, Mozambique, and Guinea-Bissau comes to an end; the Soviets fly Cuban troops to Angola; Congress passes the Jackson-Vanik Amendment, tying Soviet-American trade with Soviet willingness to increase Jewish emigration from the USSR; Nixon resigns after the Watergate scandal, and Gerald Ford becomes president.

1975
The Soviet Union rejects the U.S.-Soviet trade agreement because of the Jackson-Vanik Amendment; South Vietnam and Cambodia fall to Communists; the United States, Soviet Union, and thirty-three other nations sign the Helsinki Accords, calling for more contact between East and West and increased respect for human rights.

1976
The Soviet Union sends Cuban troops to support the Marxist-Leninist faction in the Angolan civil war; the pro-Soviet faction wins and assumes power; Chinese leader Mao Tse-tung dies; Jimmy Carter is elected president.

1977
Carter urges dissidents in the Soviet Union to demand greater freedom; the Soviet Union denounces U.S. interference in its internal affairs.

1978
Coups bring Marxist-Leninist regimes to power in Afghanistan and South Yemen.

1979
Chinese leader Deng Xiaoping visits the United States; China and the United States establish formal diplomatic relations; the United

States and Soviet Union sign the SALT II treaty at the Carter-Brezhnev summit in Vienna; Marxist Sandinistas come to power in Nicaragua; the Soviet Union sends troops into Afghanistan to strengthen Communist rule and combat Islamic rebels.

1980
Carter imposes economic sanctions on the USSR and announces that the United States will boycott the 1980 Moscow Olympics; the president proclaims the Carter Doctrine, committing the United States to the defense of the Persian Gulf; a workers' strike in Poland gains bargaining rights for the independent trade union Solidarity; Ronald Reagan is elected president.

1981
Reagan says that limited nuclear war in Europe is possible; a mass antinuclear movement develops in Europe, opposing NATO deployment of intermediate-range nuclear missiles; Reagan initiates U.S. military buildup; the United States begins a covert aid program for Contra rebels fighting the Nicaraguan government.

1983
Reagan proposes the Strategic Defense Initiative, a complex system of defenses against nuclear missiles; the Soviet Union shoots down a Korean Airlines passenger plane that strays over Soviet territory, claiming it was on a spy mission; the United States sends troops to Grenada to oust its Marxist-Leninist government; the United States begins deploying missiles in Europe; Soviets walk out of talks on intermediate-range nuclear forces (INF).

1984
Reagan visits China and agrees to sell weapons to China; the Soviet Union boycotts the Los Angeles Olympics.

1985
President Reagan proclaims the Reagan Doctrine of support for anti-Communist rebels fighting against Marxist governments; Mikhail Gorbachev comes to power in the Soviet Union; Reagan and Gorbachev meet at Geneva.

1986
Gorbachev calls for far-reaching reforms in the USSR and reduces economic support of Soviet satellites, including Cuba; the world's worst nuclear accident occurs at Chernobyl in the Soviet Republic

of Ukraine; Reagan and Gorbachev hold a summit at Reykjavik, Iceland, coming very close to an agreement to eliminate all nuclear weapons.

1987
Reagan and Gorbachev meet in Washington, D.C., and sign the INF Treaty, banning all intermediate-range nuclear weapons.

1988
The United States and Soviet Union reach an agreement on Soviet withdrawal from Afghanistan; Gorbachev renounces the Brezhnev Doctrine, thus allowing greater freedom to the countries of Eastern Europe, and begins other political reforms within the Soviet Union; Reagan holds a summit with Gorbachev in Moscow; George Bush is elected president.

1989
The Chinese government crushes a democracy movement at Tiananmen Square; free elections bring Solidarity's Lech Walesa to power in Poland, the first non-Communist government in Eastern Europe since the beginning of the Cold War; the Hungarian government permits East Germans to escape to the West through Hungary, rendering the Berlin Wall obsolete; it is torn down by jubilant crowds on November 9; Gorbachev renounces the use of force against Eastern Europeans, thus ending the Soviet empire; Communist governments in Czechoslovakia, Bulgaria, and Romania fall.

1990
Lithuania declares its independence; Gorbachev declares that the Communist Party is no longer entitled to a monopoly of power; non-Communists win elections throughout Eastern Europe; East German elections are won by conservative Christian Democrats, who favor reunification with West Germany; Bush and Gorbachev hold a summit in Washington, signing a chemical weapons agreement; Gorbachev accepts German reunification within NATO; the Soviet Union shows its first signs of breaking up.

1991
Germany is reunified; the Warsaw Pact is dissolved; a Communist coup against Gorbachev fails, leading to the demise of Communism; the Baltic republics of Estonia, Latvia, and Lithuania become independent; the Soviet Union dissolves, and Boris Yeltsin becomes president of non-Communist Russia.

FOR FURTHER READING

Dean Acheson, *Present at the Creation*. New York: W.W. Norton, 1969. A detailed and highly informative insider's account of early Cold War developments by Truman's secretary of state.

Graham Allison, *Essence of Decision: Explaining the Cuban Missile Crisis*. Boston: Little, Brown, 1971. A valuable work, studded with important and fascinating facts about the crisis, even though written long before the avalanche of information that became available after 1989.

Gar Alperovitz, *Atomic Diplomacy: Hiroshima and Potsdam*. Rev. ed. New York: Penguin, 1985. Provides a detailed argument that the decision to use the atomic bomb against Japan was motivated primarily by the desire to intimidate the Soviets rather than to defeat Japan.

Stephen E. Ambrose, *Rise to Globalism: American Foreign Policy Since 1938*. 7th ed. rev. New York: Penguin, 1993. A mildly critical study of the U.S. policy of containment.

David P. Barash, *The Arms Race and Nuclear War*. Belmont, CA: Wadsworth, 1987. An excellent comprehensive survey of nuclear issues from the physics of nuclear explosions to arms control. Useful for those with or without prior background in nuclear affairs.

James G. Blight and David A. Welch, *On the Brink: Americans and Soviets Re-examine the Cuban Missile Crisis*. New York: Hill and Wang, 1989. This book presents new information released by informed Soviet participants in the missile crisis.

Fred J. Cook, *The U-2 Incident: An American Spy Plane Downed over Russia Intensifies the Cold War*. New York: F. Watts, 1973. A brief account of a key Cold War episode in which the Soviets walked out of a summit conference in Paris in angry protest against overflight of Soviet territory by an American U-2 spy plane. This book shows how minor events could have a large impact on the course of events in the Cold War.

John Lewis Gaddis, *The Long Peace: Inquiries into the History of the Cold War*. New York: Oxford University Press, 1987. Contains keenly insightful essays on diverse Cold War topics primarily in the 1940s and 1950s by one of the leading historians on the Cold War.

————, *The United States and the Origins of the Cold War, 1941–1947*. New York: Columbia University Press, 1972. A thoughtful, balanced, and thorough analysis of the Cold War's origins.

Derek Benjamin Heater, *The Cold War*. New York: Bookwright, 1989. A very brief overview history of the Cold War; comprehensive but highly general.

George C. Herring, *America's Longest War*. New York: Wiley, 1988. A short but comprehensive and highly readable history of American involvement in Vietnam.

Stanley C. Karnow, *Vietnam, a History: The First Complete Account of Vietnam at War*. New York: Viking, 1983. A highly regarded one-volume history of the Vietnam War. The basis for a multipart PBS documentary.

George F. Kennan, *Memoirs, 1925–1950*. Boston: Little, Brown, 1967. An informed account of the early Cold War by distinguished Sovietologist, policymaker, and intellectual godfather of containment policy.

Nikita Khrushchev, *Khrushchev Remembers*. Boston: Little, Brown, 1970. A lively and generally accurate account by the ebullient Soviet leader, offering a Soviet perspective on the Cold War.

Henry A. Kissinger, *Years of Upheaval*. Boston: Little, Brown, 1982. This second volume of superb, if self-serving, memoirs focuses almost exclusively on the events of 1973 and the author's role as secretary of state.

Michael Kort, *The Cold War*. Brookfield, CT: Millbrook, 1994. Well-chosen photographs illustrate this clearly written 160-page history of the entire Cold War. A good introduction.

Walter LaFeber, *America, Russia, and the Cold War, 1945–1990*. 6th ed. New York: McGraw-Hill, 1991. A short, readable history of the Cold War; consistently critical of U.S. policy.

Deborah Welch Larson, *Origins of Containment*. Princeton, NJ: Princeton University Press, 1985. An analysis of the Cold War's origins, with heavy emphasis on the psychological factors operating on the American side.

John Newhouse, *Cold Dawn: The Story of SALT*. New York: Holt, Rinehart, and Winston, 1973. The best account of SALT I, written with a journalist's flair.

Thomas G. Paterson, *Kennedy's Quest for Victory: American Foreign Policy, 1961–1963*. New York: Oxford University Press, 1989. A collection of ten informative essays critiquing Kennedy's foreign policy on Cuba, Vietnam, NATO, China, and other issues.

David Pietrusza, *The End of the Cold War*. San Diego: Lucent Books, 1995. An insightful analysis of the events leading to the end of the Cold War and the personalities of the key players as they grappled with difficult and contentious issues.

Richard Smoke, *National Security and the Nuclear Dilemma*. 3rd ed. New York: Holmes and Meier, 1985. A clearly written scholarly study of the impact of nuclear weapons on the Cold War.

Conrad R. Stein, *The Great Red Scare*. Parsippany, NJ: New Discovery Books, 1998. Portrays the deep fears in the United States of the Soviets and of Soviet spies in the earliest phases of the Cold War; describes in detail the phenomenon of McCarthyism.

Richard Steins, *The Postwar Years: The Cold War and the Atomic Age, 1950–1959*. New York: Twenty-First Century Books, 1993. An examination of the darkest, most tense period of the Cold War and of the impact of nuclear weapons.

Strobe Talbott, *Deadly Gambits*. New York: Knopf, 1984. A lively insider's account of arms control negotiations under Reagan on both strategic nuclear weapons and intermediate-range nuclear forces. This book emphasizes the sharp disagreements between Reagan's advisers and the ill-informed president's inability to reign in the debates.

James A. Warren, *Cold War: The American Crusade Against World Communism, 1945–1991*. New York: Lothrop, Lee, and Shepard Books, 1996. A solid introduction to America's Soviet policy from the beginning to the end of the Cold War. A very readable and fairly comprehensive book for its one-hundred-page length.

Works Consulted

Books

Michael R. Beschloss and Strobe Talbott, *At the Highest Levels: The Inside Story of the End of the Cold War*. Boston: Little, Brown, 1993. A fascinating and well-informed insider's account of the end of the Cold War by a distinguished historian, Beschloss, and journalist, Talbott.

Bernard Brodie, *The Absolute Weapon*. New York: Harcourt, Brace, 1946. One of the first inquiries into the effects of nuclear weapons on national strategies. Brodie's conclusion that nuclear weapons can do nothing but deter an adversary from using nuclear weapons is still widely cited.

Robert Conquest, *The Great Terror: A Reassessment*. New York: Oxford University Press, 1990. Provides thorough documentation and analysis of Stalin's purges and show trials and a moving account of the suffering inflicted on tens of millions who were exiled, jailed, or killed under the orders of Stalin.

——, *The Harvest of Sorrow: Soviet Collectivization and the Terror-Famine*. New York: Oxford University Press, 1986. The best account in print of this harrowing period in Soviet history.

Cecil V. Crabb Jr., *The Doctrines of American Foreign Policy: Their Meaning, Role, and Future*. Baton Rouge: Louisiana State University Press, 1982. A detailed analysis of eight presidential doctrines from Monroe to Carter. Six of the eight are directly or indirectly aimed at the Soviet Union.

W. Raymond Duncan and Carolyn McGiffert Ekedahl, *Moscow and the Third World Under Gorbachev*. Boulder, CO: Westview, 1990. A well-researched early account of Gorbachev's policies toward key regions and countries. The authors document their argument that Gorbachev's policies represented a fundamental departure from earlier policies.

Raymond L. Garthoff, *Détente and Confrontation: American-Soviet Relations from Nixon to Reagan*. Washington, DC: Brookings, 1985. A massive, heavily researched study of U.S.-Soviet relations from 1969 to 1984. Consistently critical of U.S. policy, but highly informative.

Louis J. Halle, *The Cold War as History*. New York: Harper, 1967. An early, interpretive history of the Cold War. Halle puts the blame for the East-West conflict squarely on the Soviets.

John B. Harris and Eric Markusen, eds., *Nuclear Weapons and the Threat of Nuclear War*. New York: Harcourt Brace Jovanovich, 1986. An anthology comprising essays on the moral, political, and strategic controversies surrounding nuclear weapons.

Mark Heller, *The Soviet Invasion of Afghanistan: Motivations and Implications*. Tel Aviv: Center for Strategic Studies, 1980. A brief and very early account of the invasion.

Edwin P. Hoyt, *America's Wars and Military Encounters from Colonial Times to the Present*. New York: Da Capo, 1988. A brief but colorful and reasonably comprehensive history of all of America's wars, including Vietnam and Korea.

William G. Hyland, *The Cold War: Fifty Years of Conflict*. New York: Random House, 1991. An informed and insightful interpretive account of the Cold War by a highly respected scholar and statesman.

Charles W. Kegley Jr. and Eugene R. Wittkopf, *American Foreign Policy: Pattern and Process*. New York: St. Martin's, 1996. A widely used college text providing a comprehensive introduction to the major issues of American foreign policy and the process by which it is made.

——, eds., *Perspectives on American Foreign Policy*. New York: St. Martin's, 1983. Complementing the text by the same authors, this anthology of thirty-two readings covers topics on the substance, process, and theory of American foreign policy.

Henry A. Kissinger, *White House Years*. Boston: Little, Brown, 1979. A massive account and defense of the Nixon-Kissinger foreign policy (1969–1972) by Nixon's national security adviser. This book is lucidly written, frequently philosophical, and occasionally humorous.

Melvyn P. Leffler, *A Preponderance of Power: National Security, the Truman Administration, and the Cold War*. Palo Alto, CA: Stanford University Press, 1992. A lengthy and thoroughly researched study of Truman's Soviet policy; the definitive work on the subject.

Ralph B. Levering, *The Cold War, 1945–1987*. Arlington Heights, IL: Harlan Davidson, 1988. A critical history of America's Soviet policy; short and readable.

Herbert M. Levine and Jean Edward Smith, eds., *The Conduct of American Foreign Policy Debated*. New York: McGraw-Hill, 1990. This volume presents twenty-three pairs of pro-con essays on U.S. foreign policy.

Guenter Lewy, *America in Vietnam*. Oxford, England: Oxford University Press, 1978. An excellent study of America's war effort, especially in assessing the strengths and weaknesses of counterinsurgency warfare and the use of airpower.

David McCullough, *Truman*. New York: Touchstone, 1992. An engaging biography of President Truman by a best-selling author.

Michael McGwire, *Perestroika and Soviet National Security*. Washington, DC: Brookings, 1991. A fairly arcane text written by and for specialists.

James A. Nathan and James K. Oliver, *United States Foreign Policy and World Order*, 4th ed. Glenview, IL: Scott, Foresman, 1989. A comprehensive history of American foreign policy following World War II, devoting much space to analysis of U.S.-Soviet relations.

John Newhouse, *War and Peace in the Nuclear Age*. New York: Alfred A. Knopf, 1989. A well-written study of America's Soviet policy from Truman to Reagan. A combination of anecdotes and analysis makes the book both informative and engaging.

Joseph S. Nye Jr., ed., *The Making of America's Soviet Policy*. New Haven, CT: Yale University Press, 1984. A highly useful collection of essays by distinguished scholars covering the process by which America's Soviet policy was made.

Don Oberdorfer, *The Turn: From the Cold War to a New Era, the United States and the Soviet Union, 1983–1990*. New York: Poseidon, 1991. An informed and engaging journalistic account of the transformation of the U.S.-Soviet relationship from deep hostility to broad cooperation; heavy on anecdotes and personalities.

Thomas G. Paterson, J. Garry Clifford, and Kenneth J. Hagan, *American Foreign Relations: A History*. 4th ed. Lexington, MA: D.C. Heath, 1995. With abundant quotations, the authors present a comprehensive introduction to one hundred years of American foreign policy.

Thomas G. Paterson and Dennis Merrill, eds., *Major Problems in American Foreign Relations: Documents and Essays*. 4th ed.

Lexington, MA: D.C. Heath, 1995. A very useful anthology on American foreign policy from World War I on. Organized primarily by era, this collection combines key documents and interpretive essays.

Andrew J. Rotter, ed., *Light at the End of the Tunnel: A Vietnam War Anthology*. New York: St. Martin's, 1991. A very useful collection with thirty-nine chapters covering a broad range of military and political issues pertaining to the Vietnam War.

R.B. Smith, *An International History of the Vietnam War*. Vol. 2. *The Struggle for Southeast Asia, 1961–65*. New York: St. Martin's, 1985. Scholarly accounts of the broader regional and global context within which the Vietnam conflict developed in the early 1960s; primarily aimed at specialists.

John Spanier and Steven W. Hook, *American Foreign Policy Since World War II*. 14th ed. Washington, DC: CQ, 1998. A very popular introductory college text on American foreign policy. Provides balanced analysis and a good command of a broad range of material.

Alexis de Tocqueville, *Democracy in America*. Trans. George Lawrence. New York: Harper and Row, 1969. A perceptive view of American democracy by a French observer who toured the United States in the 1830s.

Adam B. Ulam, *Expansion and Coexistence: Soviet Foreign Policy, 1917–73*. 2nd ed. New York: Praeger, 1974. This classic study finds expansion to be the dominant motif of Soviet foreign policy.

Bernard A. Weisberger, *Cold War, Cold Peace: The United States and Russia Since 1945*. Boston: Houghton Mifflin, 1984. A useful introductory history of the Cold War, consistently critical of U.S. policy.

Daniel Yergin, *Shattered Peace: The Origins of the Cold War and the National Security State*. Boston: Houghton Mifflin, 1977. A widely used history of the origins of the Cold War. Yergin faults the United States for misconceiving and thus overreacting to the Soviet threat.

Periodicals

Vernon V. Aspaturian, "Soviet Global Power and the Correlation of Forces," *Problems in Communism*, May/June 1980.

Shahram Chubin, "U.S. Security Interests in the Persian Gulf in the 1980s," *Daedalus*, Fall 1980.

Steven R. David, "Why the Third World Matters," *International Security*, Summer 1989.

Daniel Deudney and G. John Ikenberry, "Who Won the Cold War?" *Foreign Policy*, Summer 1992.

Bruce W. Jentleson, "American Commitments in the Third World: Theory vs. Practice," *International Organization*, Autumn 1987.

Walter Lippmann, "The Cold War," *Foreign Affairs*, Spring 1987.

John Mueller, "Enough Rope," *New Republic*, July 3, 1989.

Richard Pipes, "Why the Soviet Union Thinks It Can Fight and Win a Nuclear War," *Commentary*, July 1977.

Marshall D. Shulman, "What the Russians Really Want: A Rational Response to the Soviet Nuclear Challenge," *Harper's Magazine*, April 1984.

Stephen M. Walt, "The Case for Finite Containment: Analyzing U.S. Grand Strategy," *International Security*, Summer 1989.

Weekly Compilation of Presidential Documents, January 14, 1980.

Samuel F. Wells Jr., "Sounding the Tocsin: NSC 68 and the Soviet Threat," *International Security*, Fall 1979.

Mr. X (George Kennan), "The Sources of Soviet Conduct," *Foreign Affairs*, Spring 1987.

INDEX

ABOUT THE AUTHOR

Jay Speakman has a Ph.D. in Political Science from Columbia University. He specializes in International Relations and has taught at Rutgers University, Claremont McKenna College, Pomona College, Northeastern University and the University of Massachusetts Boston. His research and teaching focus on European affairs, American foreign and national security politics and international environmental politics. Dr. Speakman lives in Barrington, Rhode Island, with his wife June and sons Jason and Adam.